I0480876

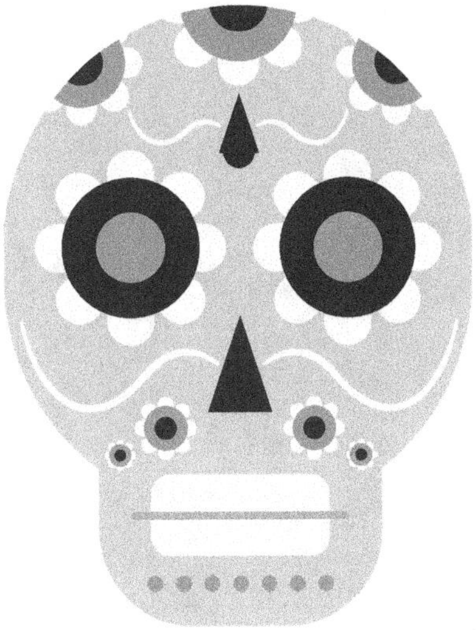

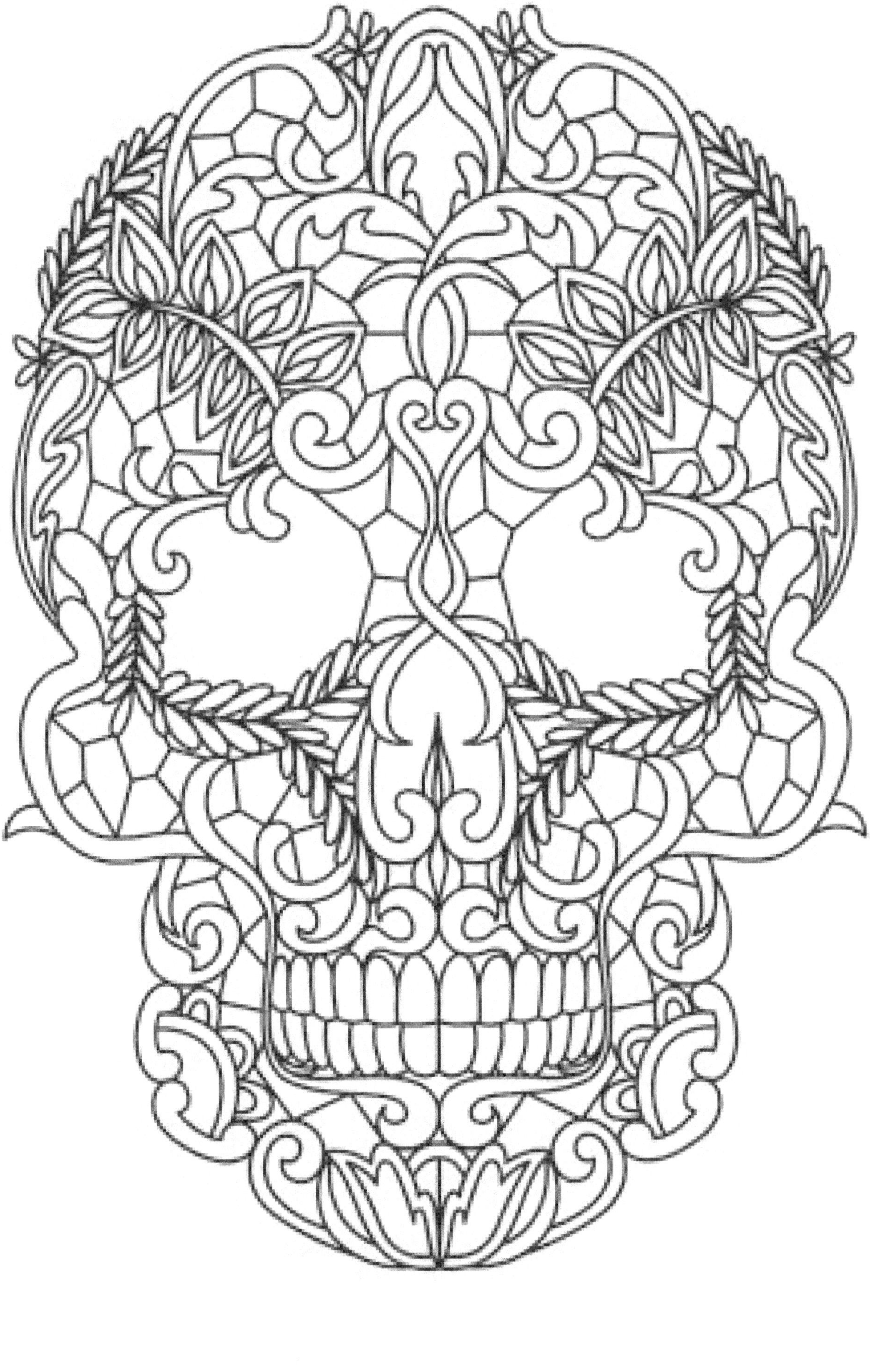

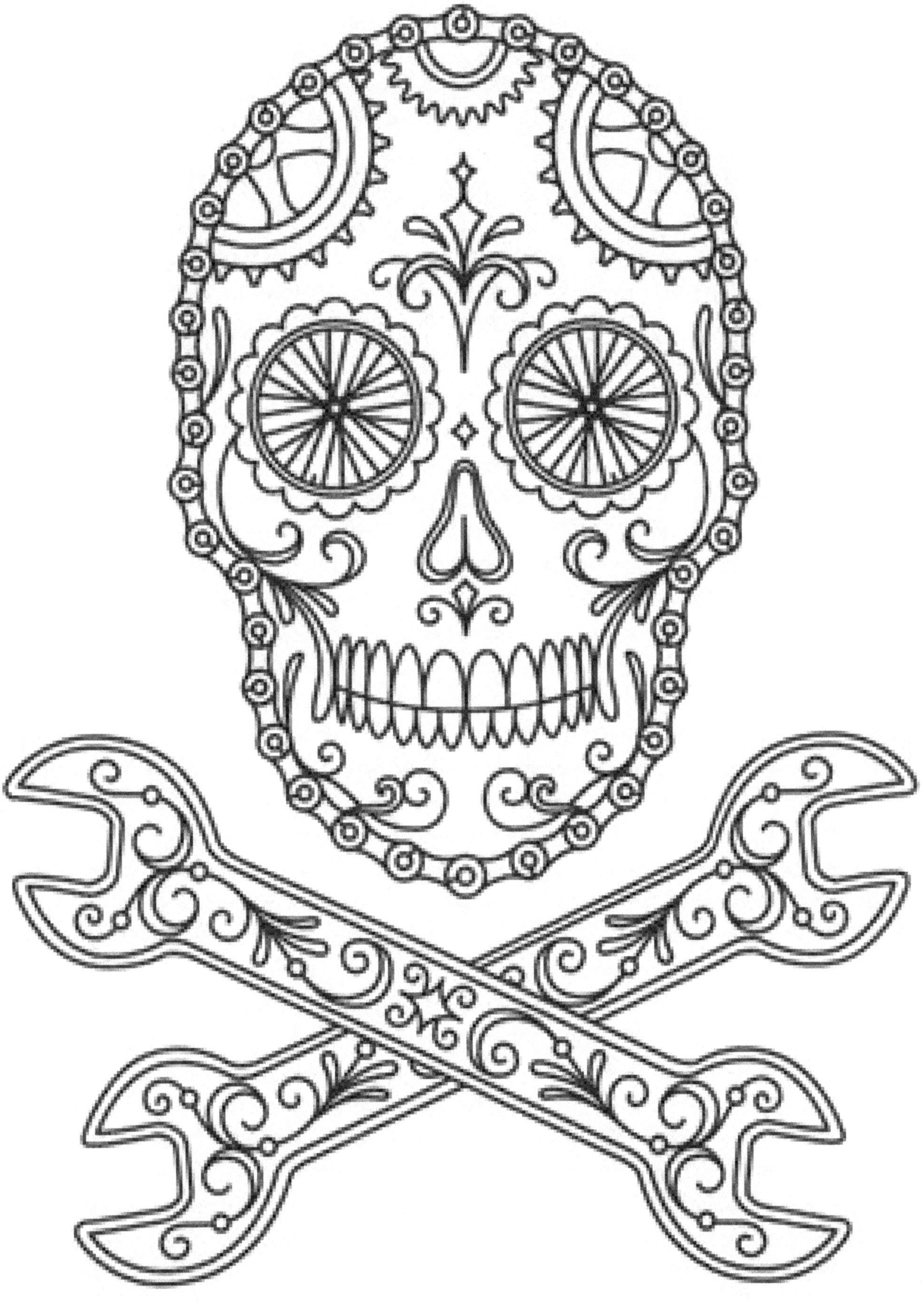

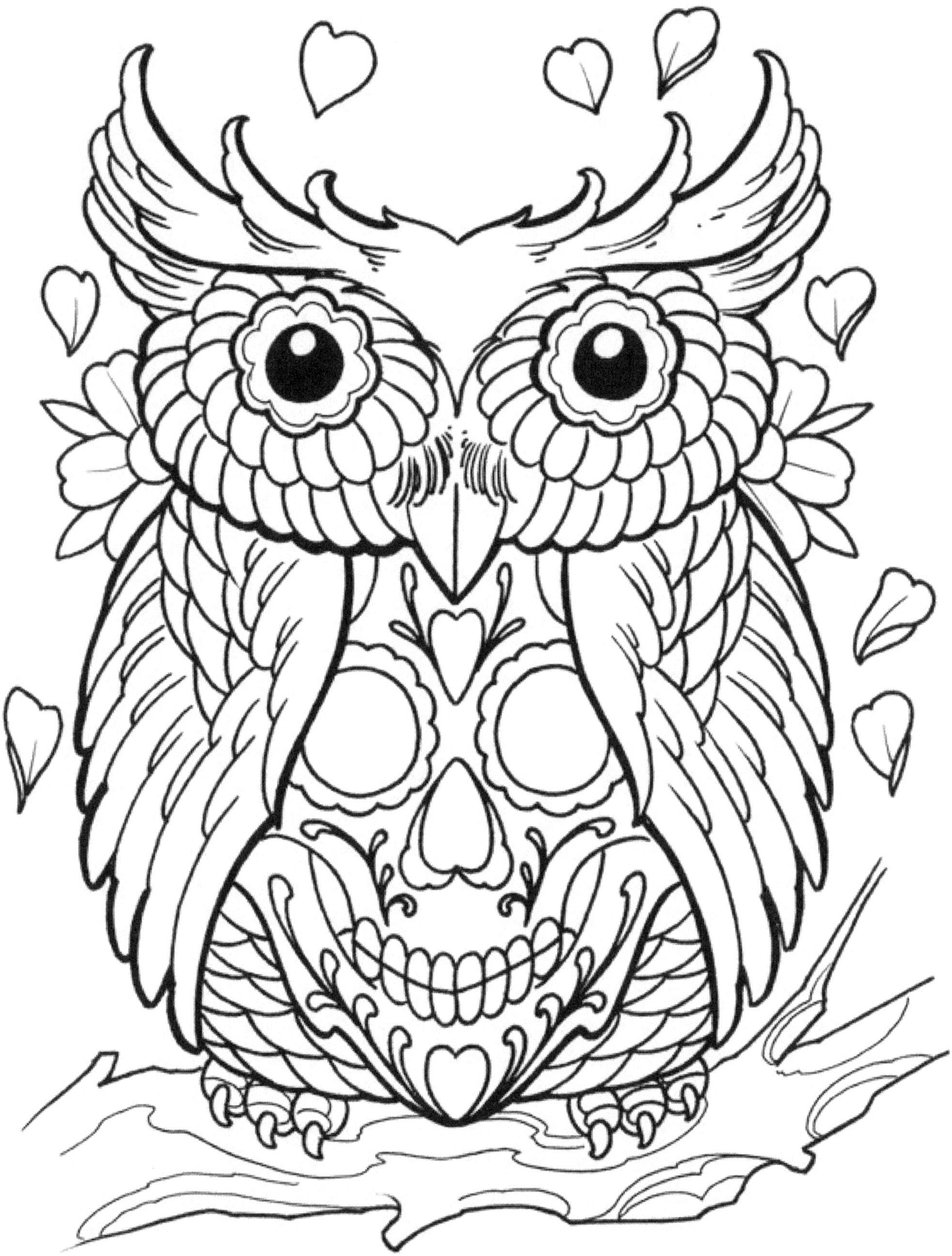

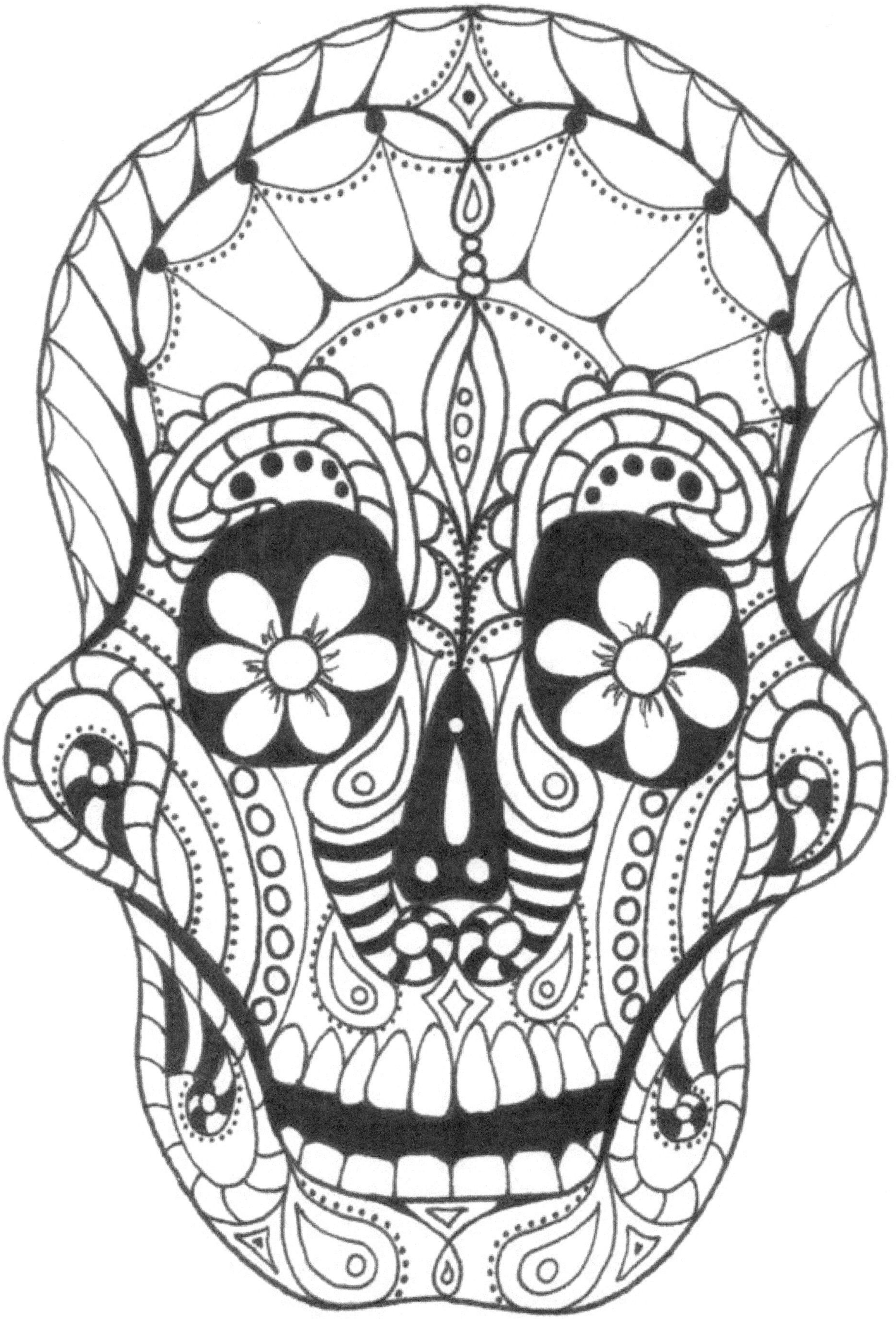

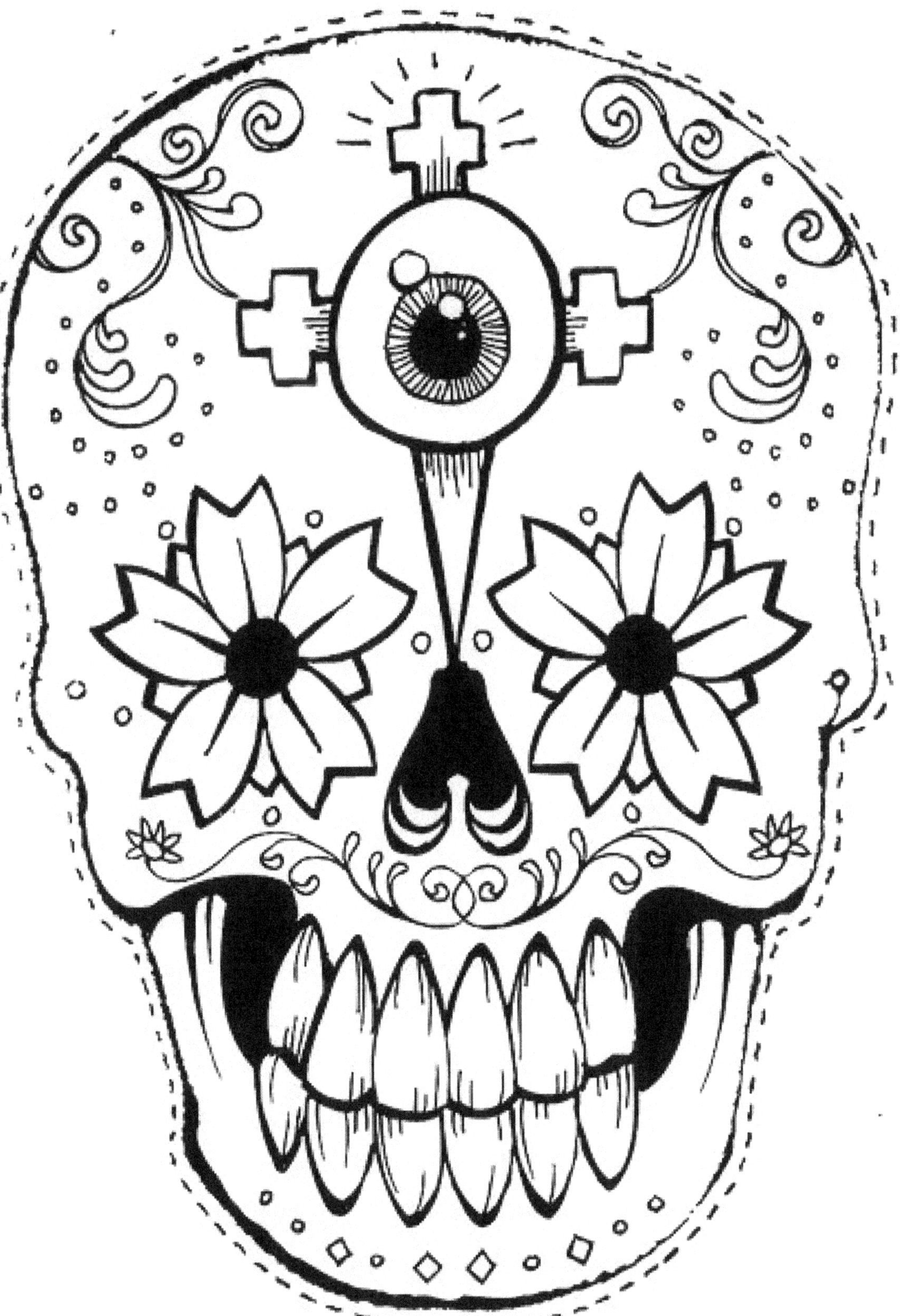

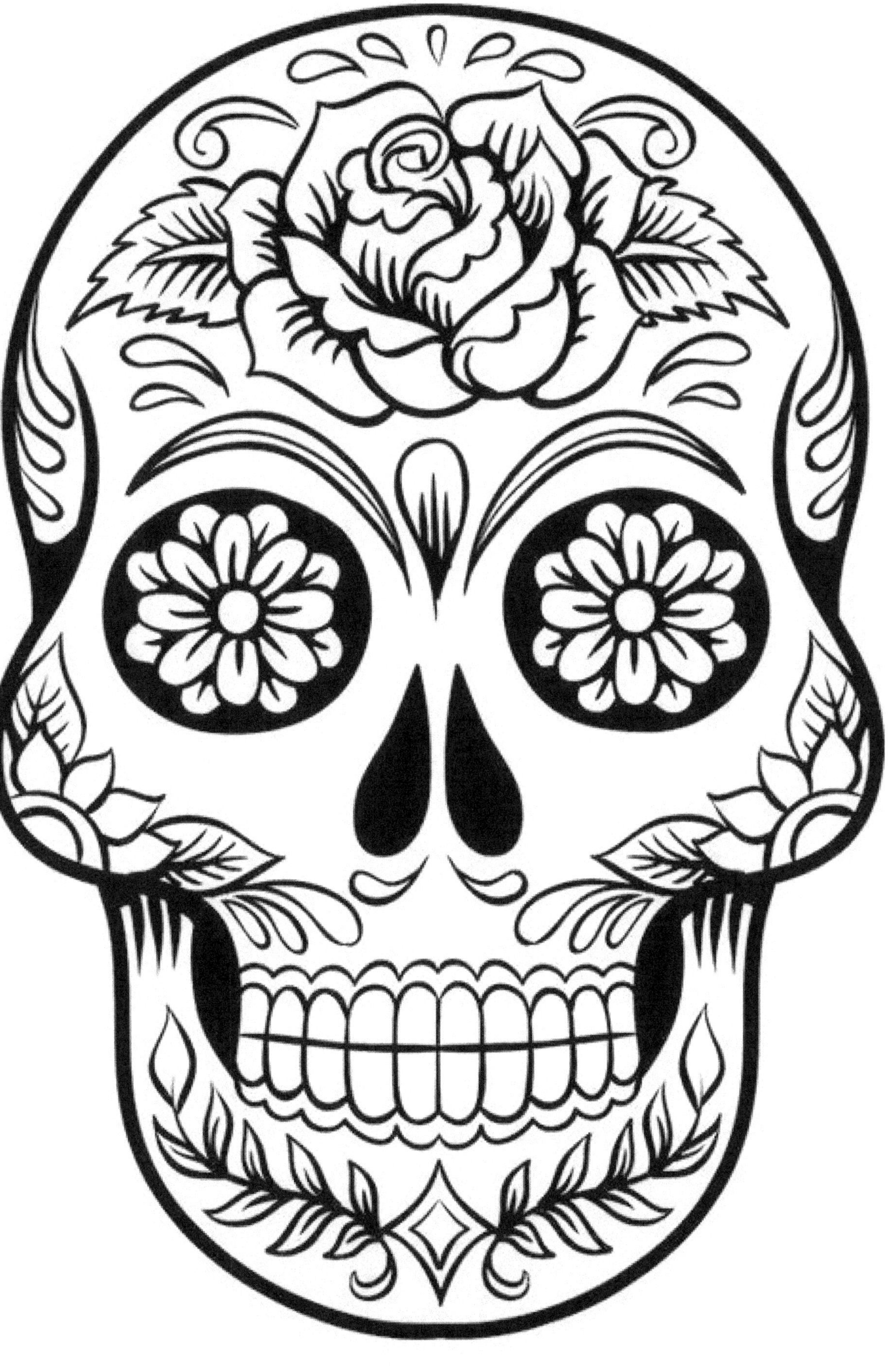

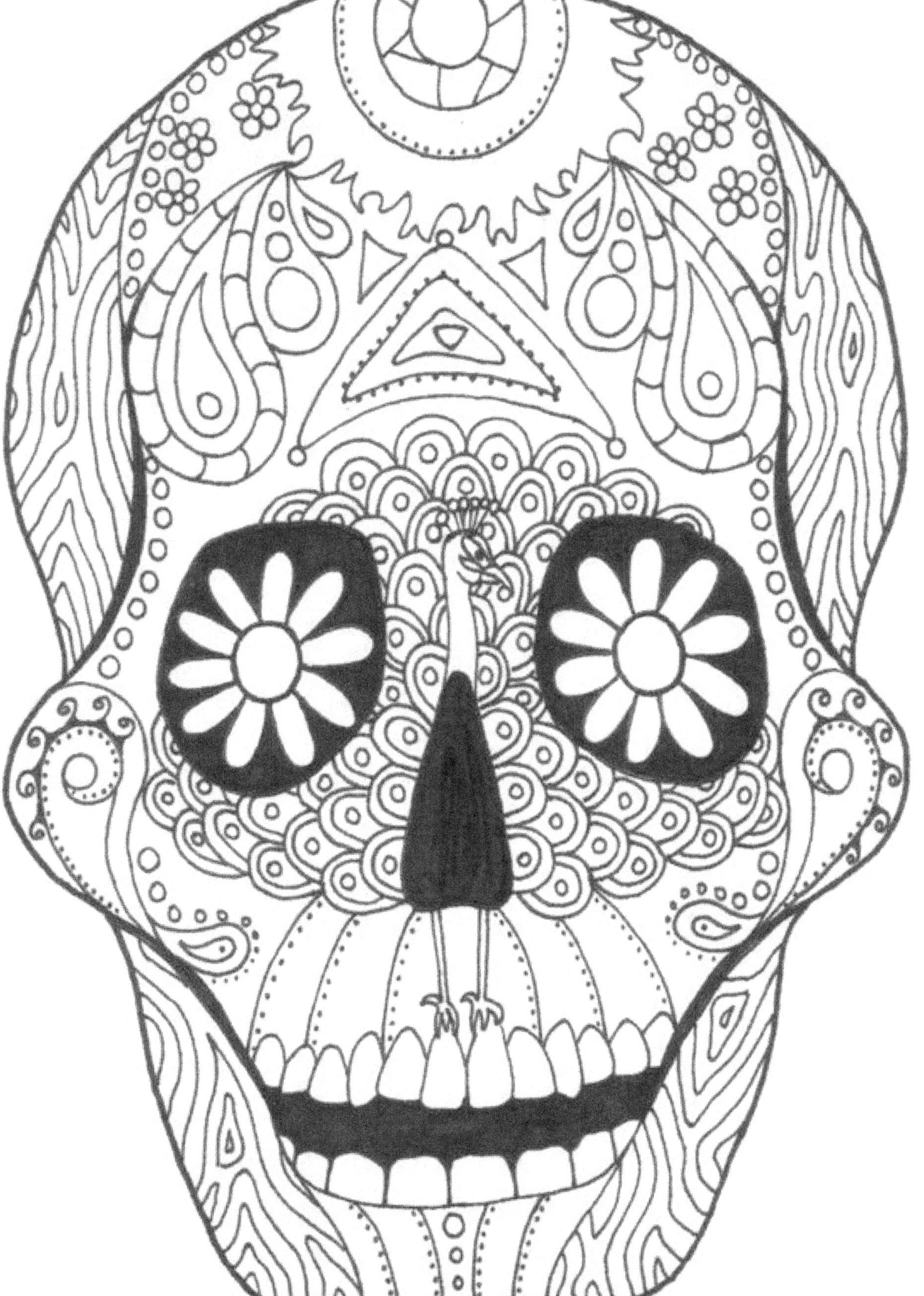

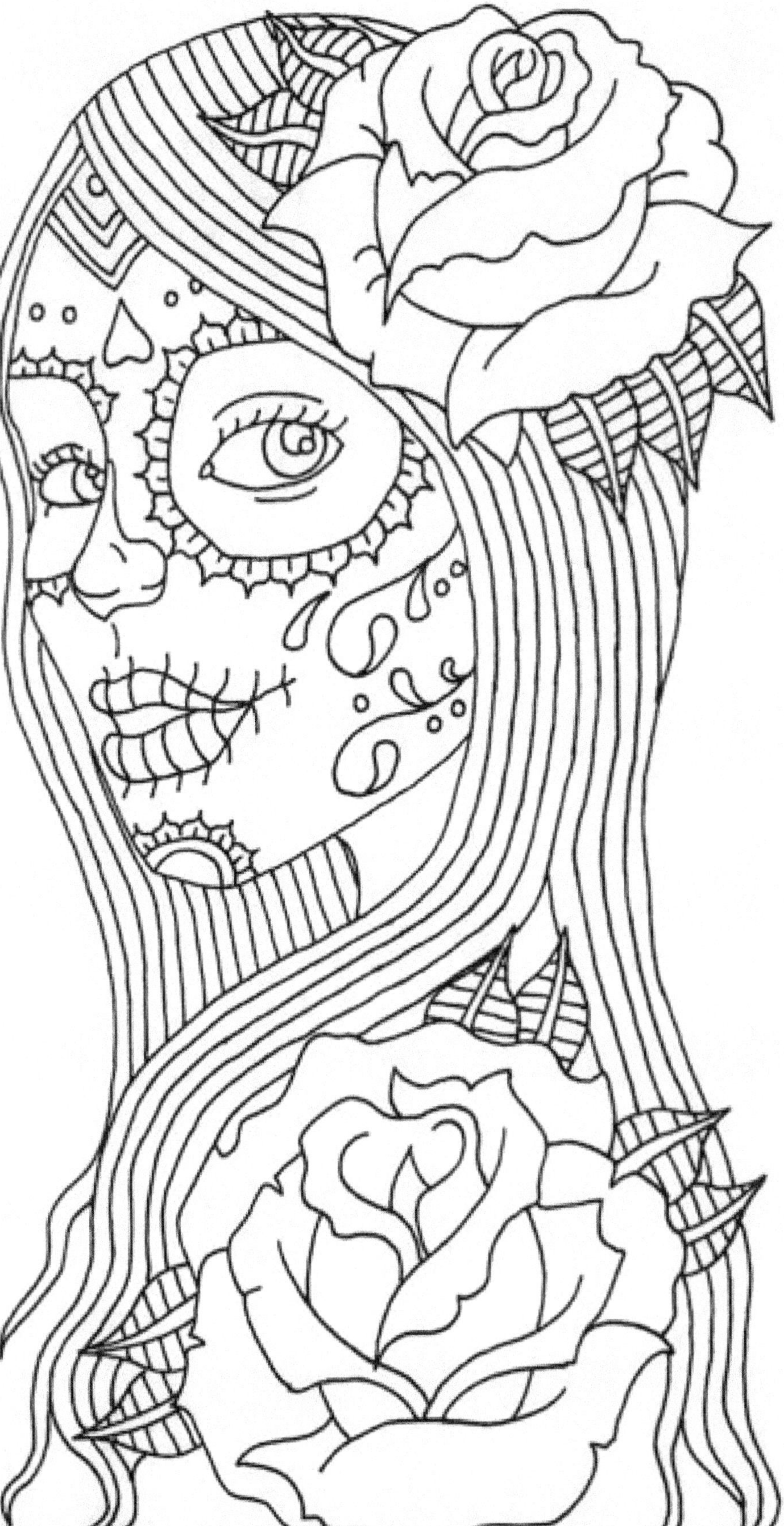

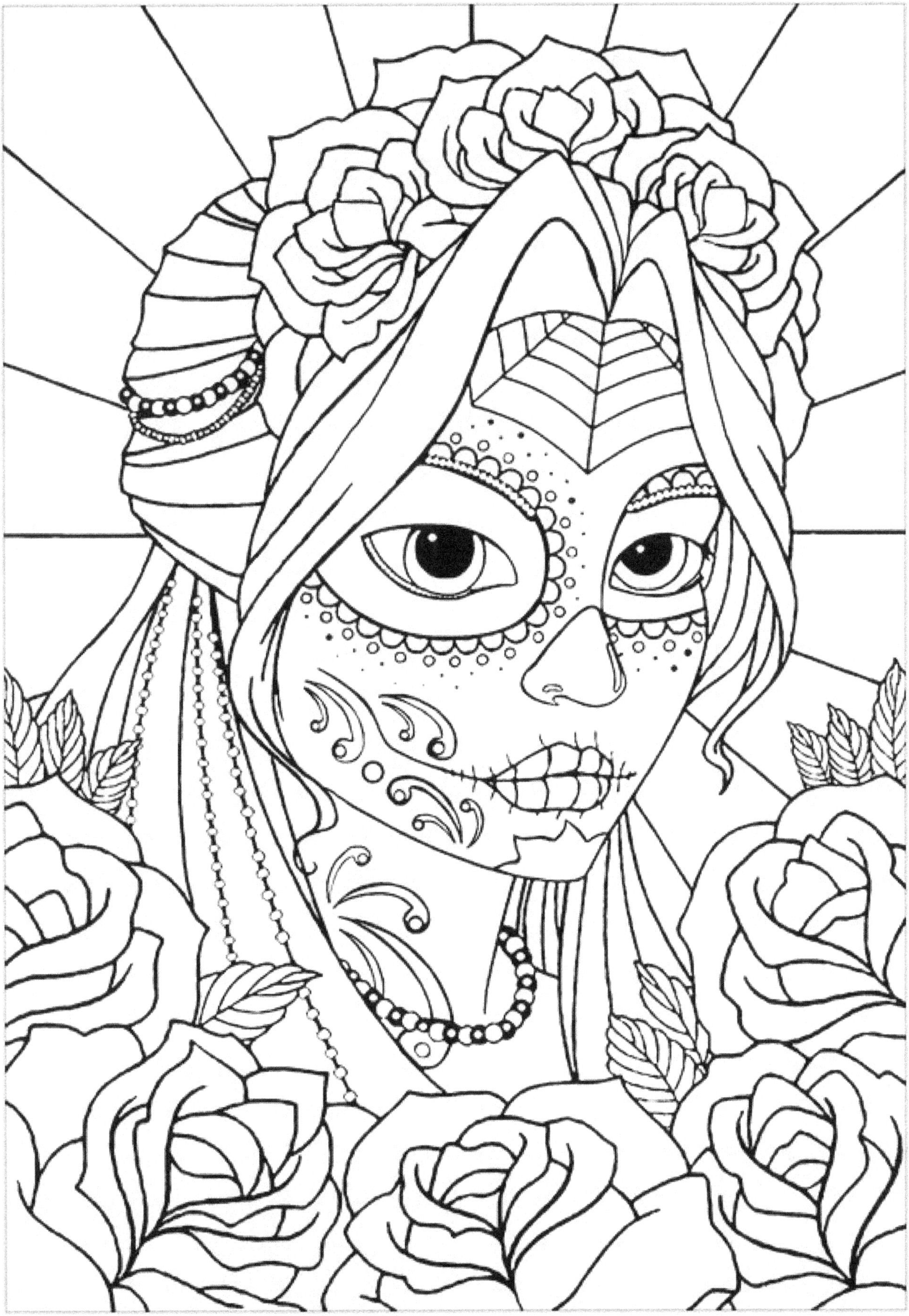

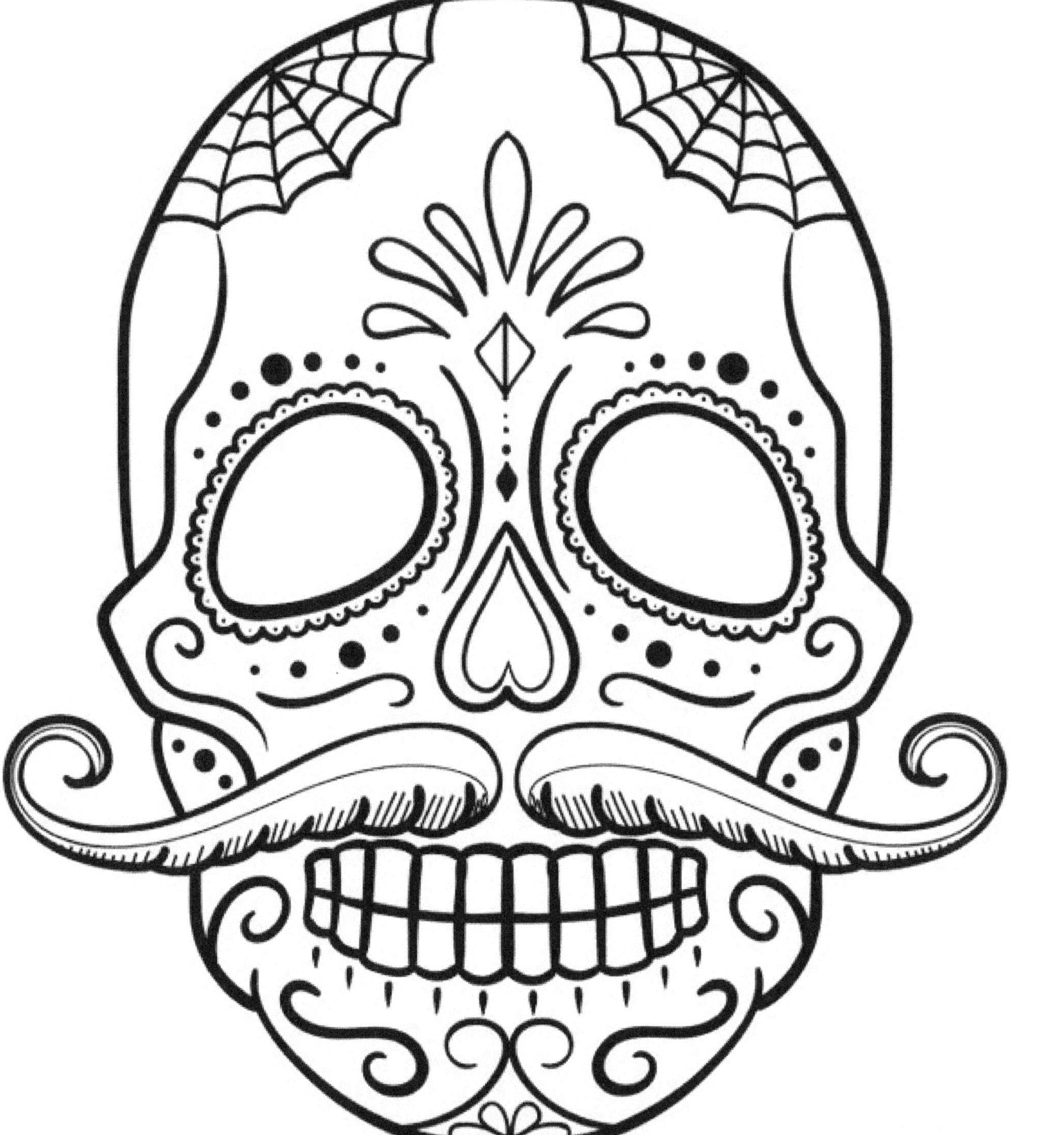

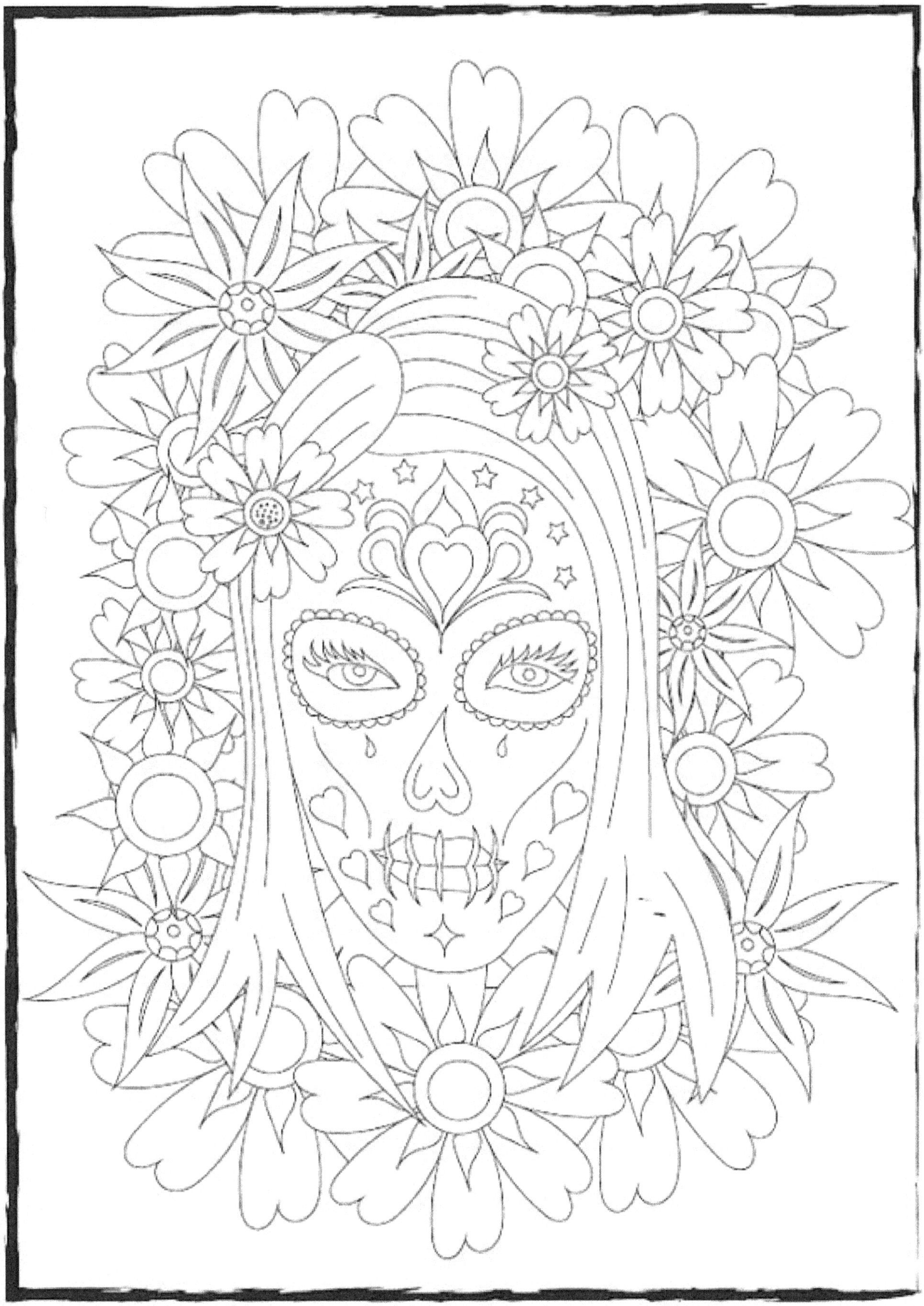

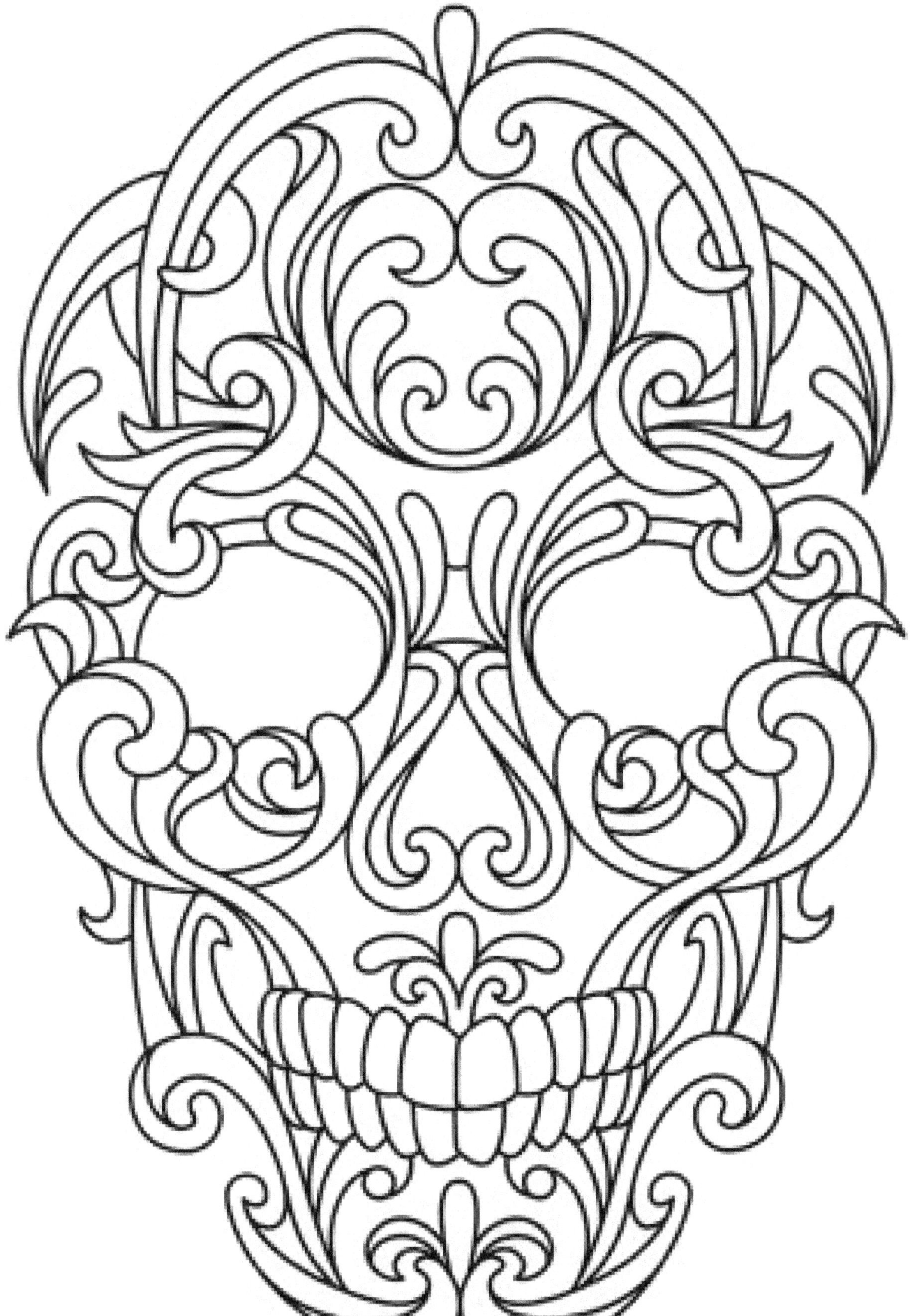

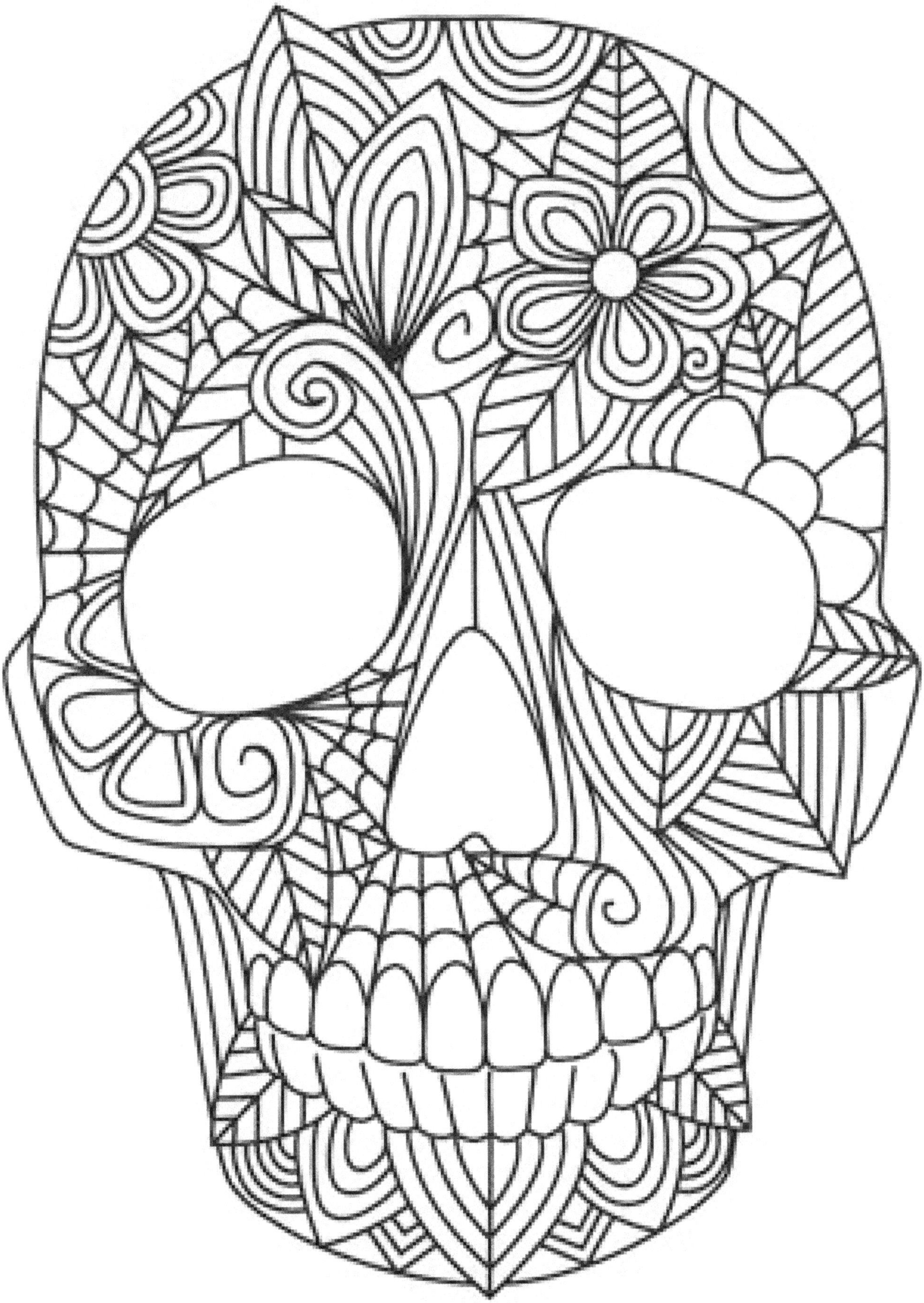

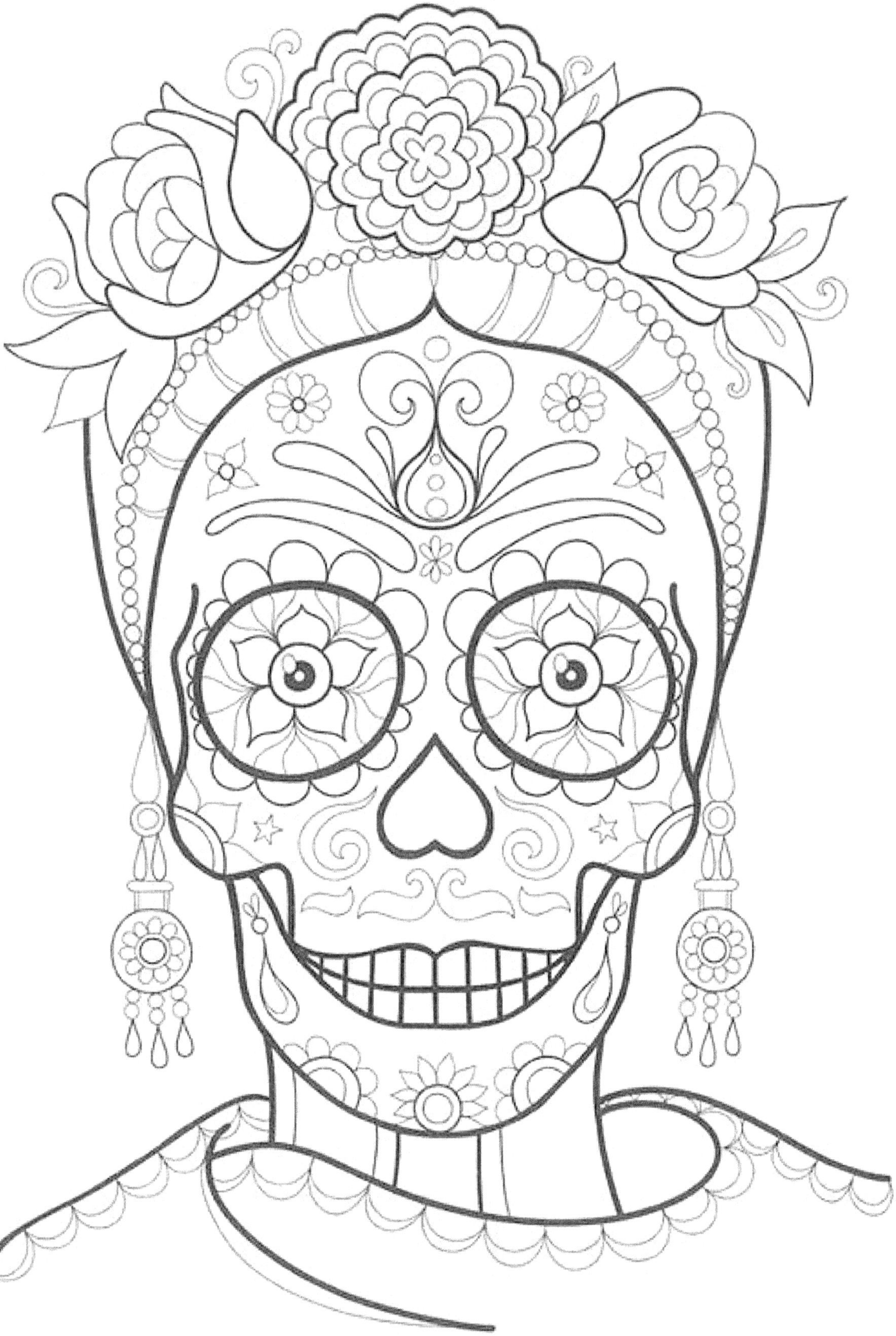

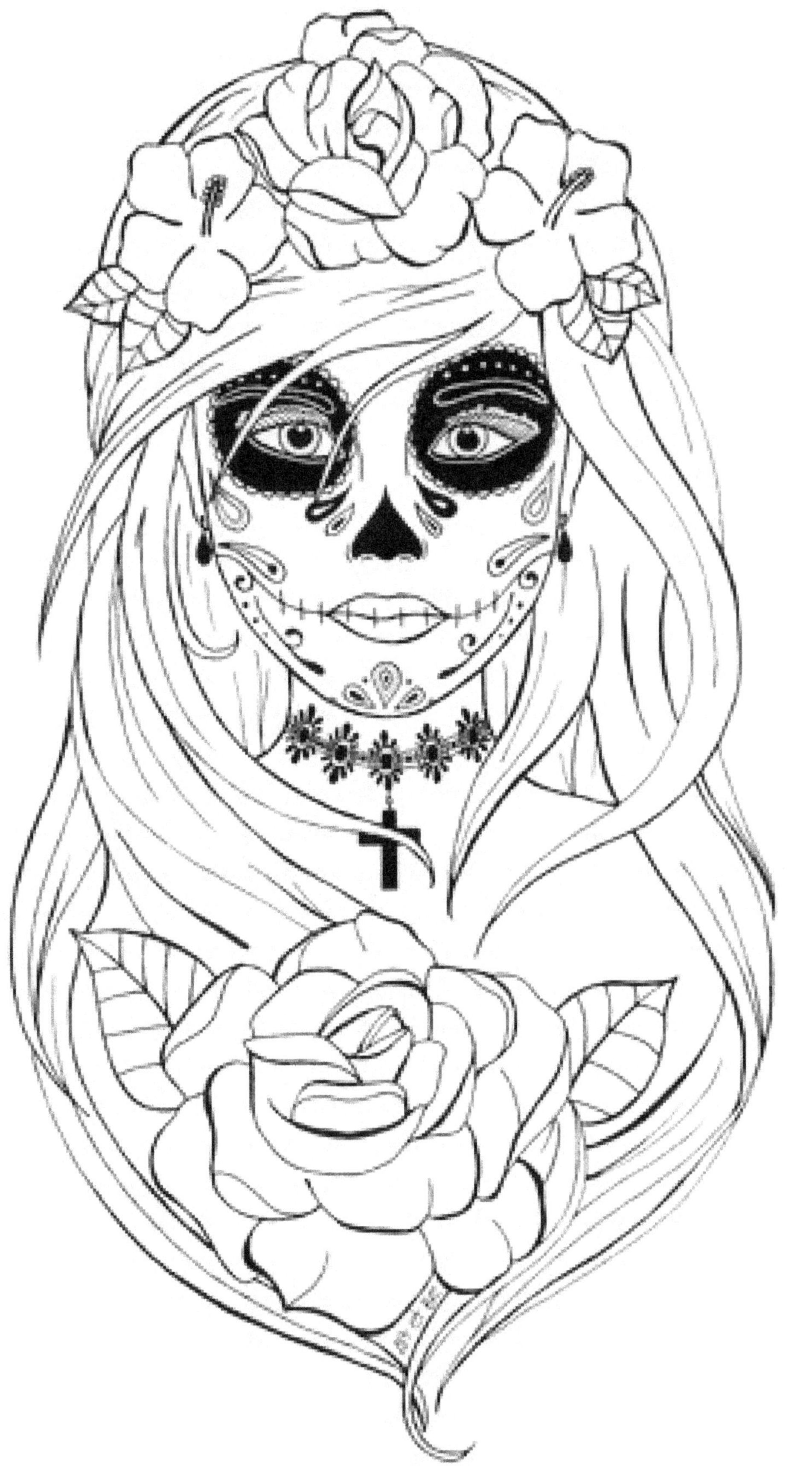

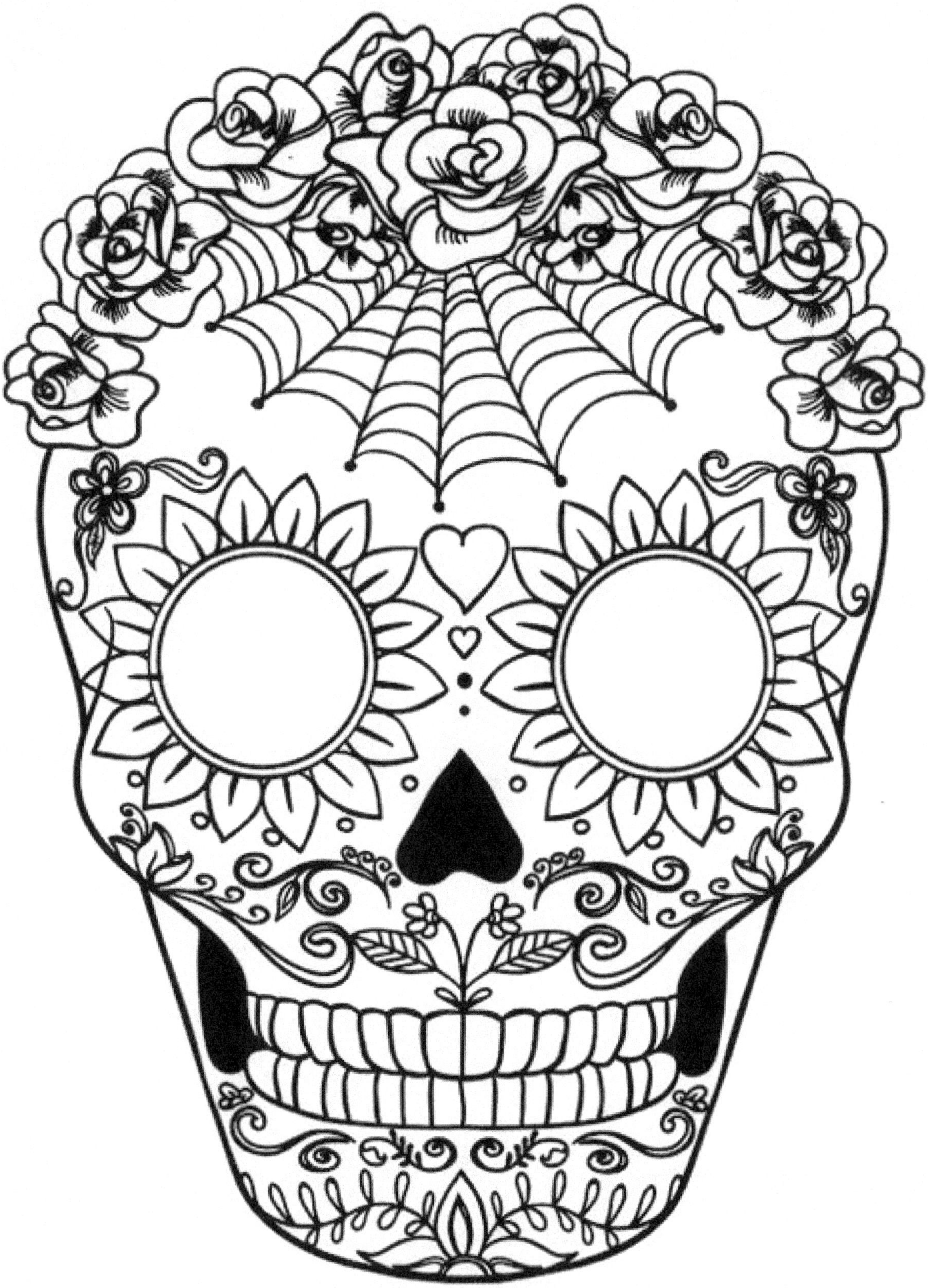

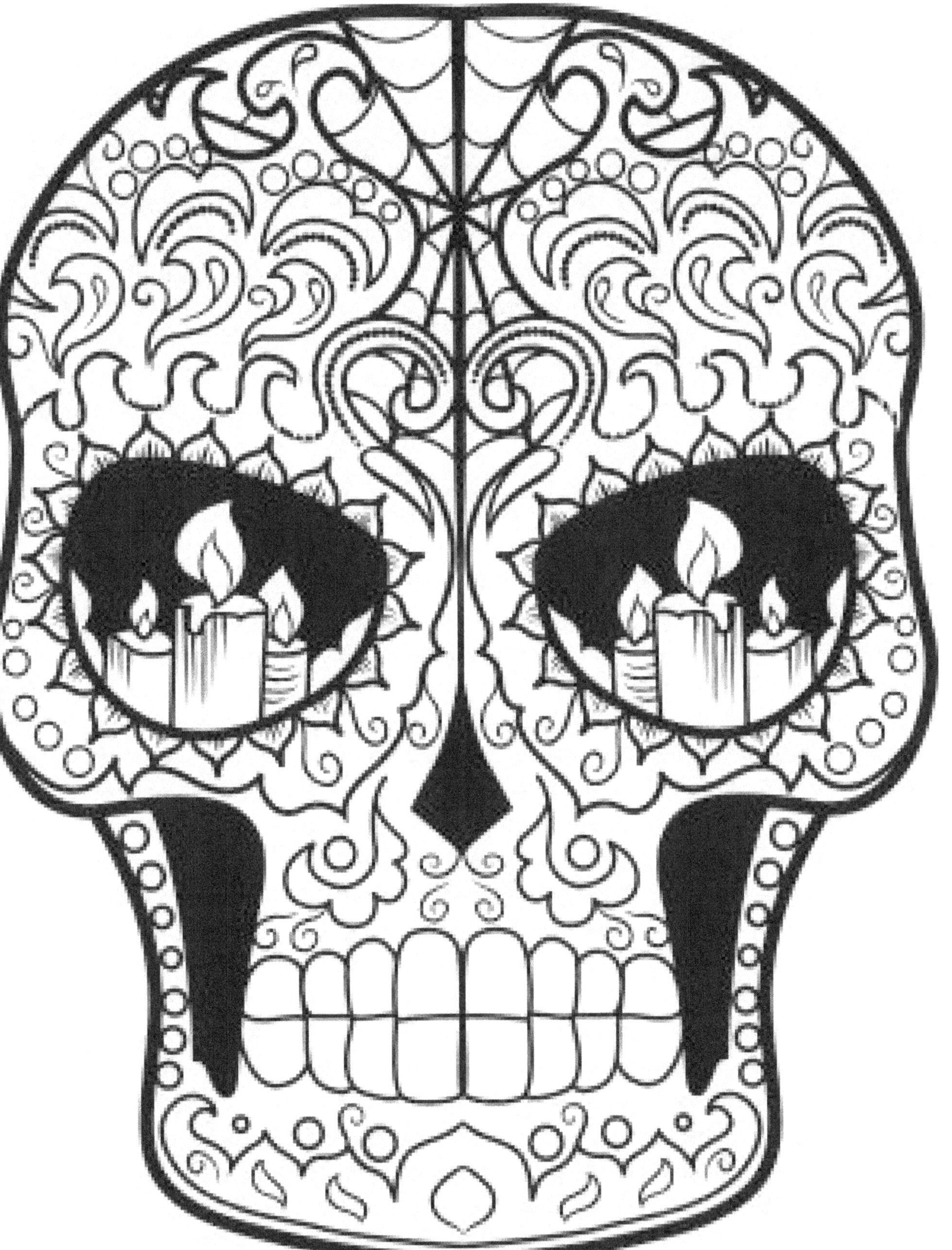

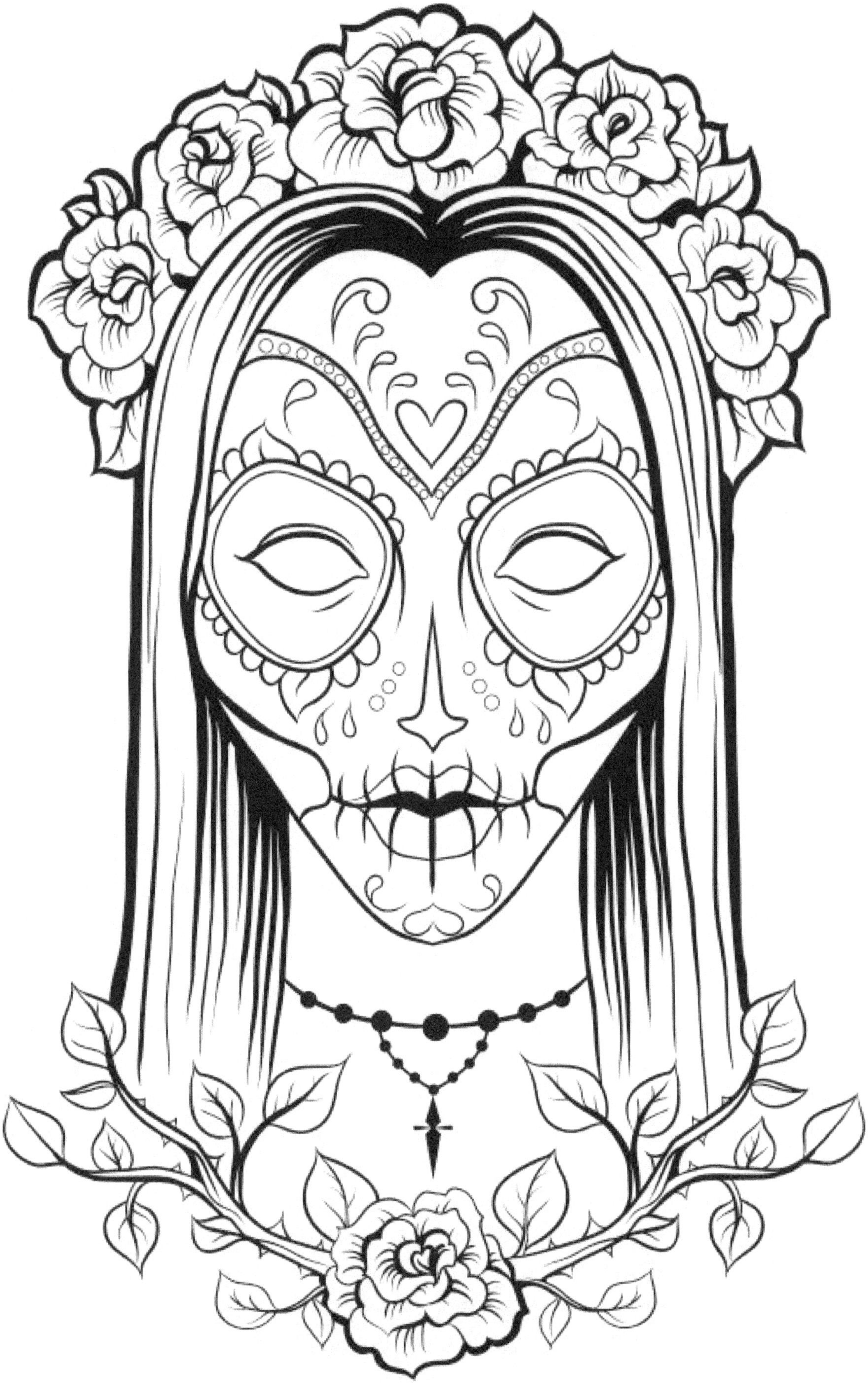

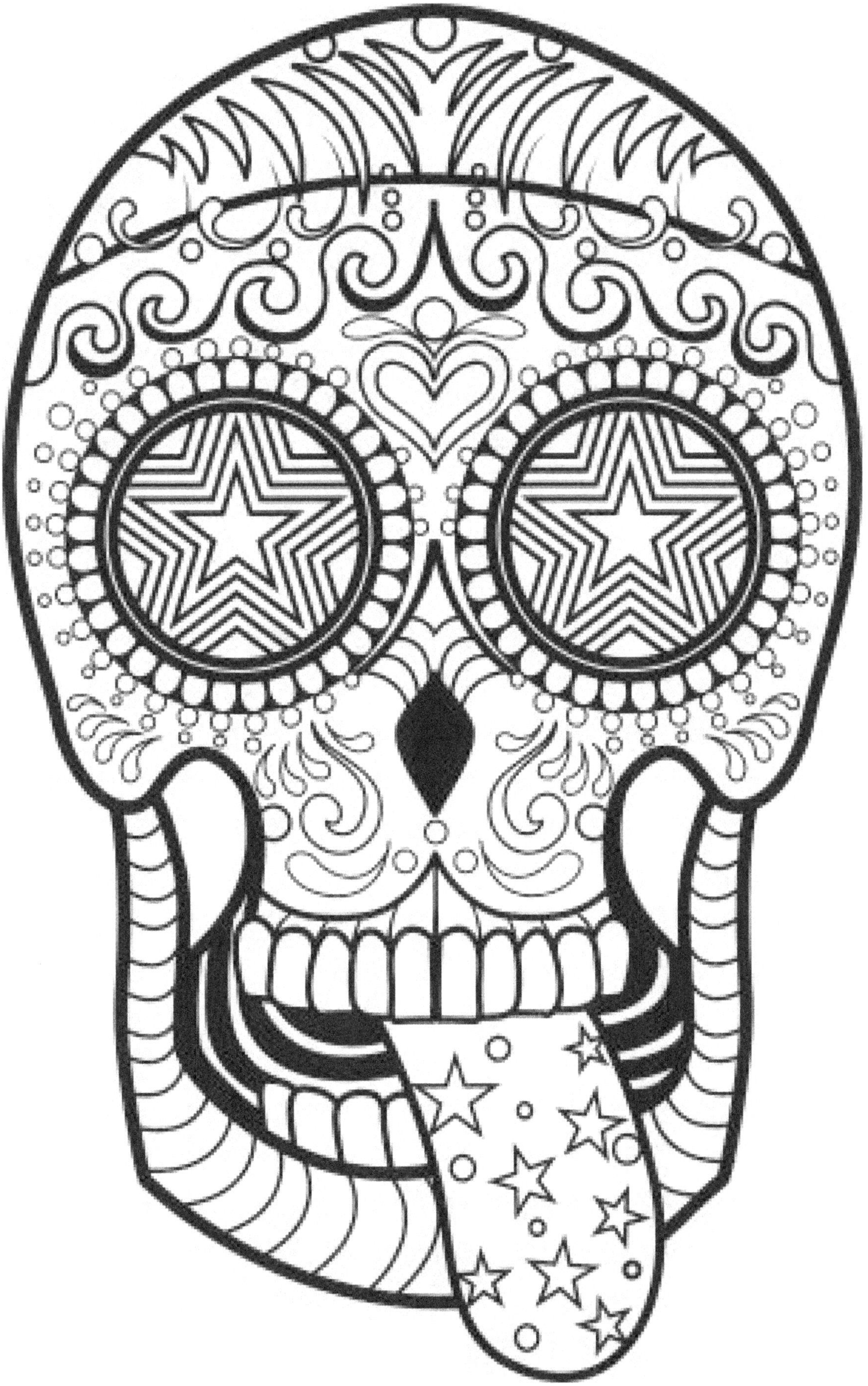

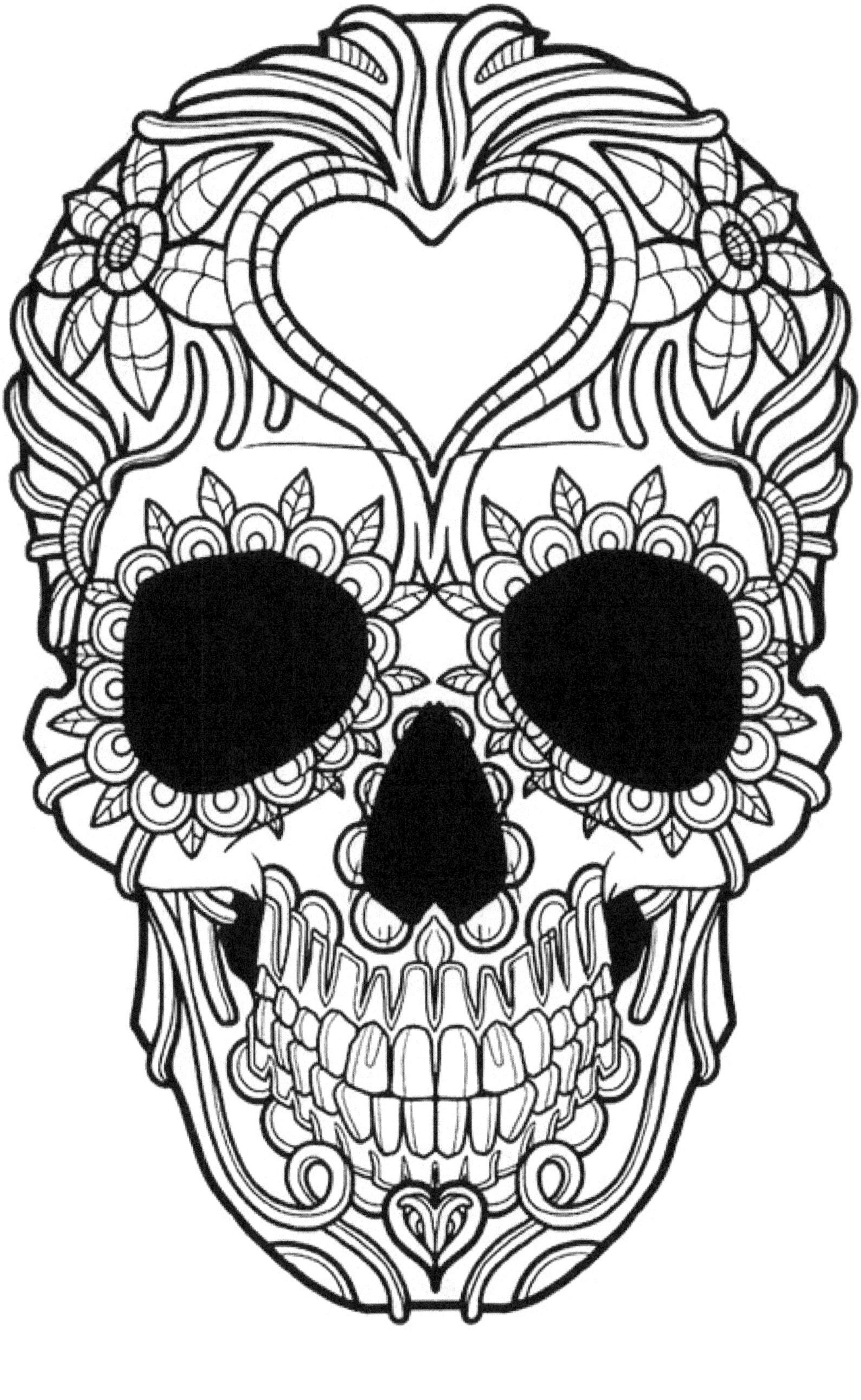

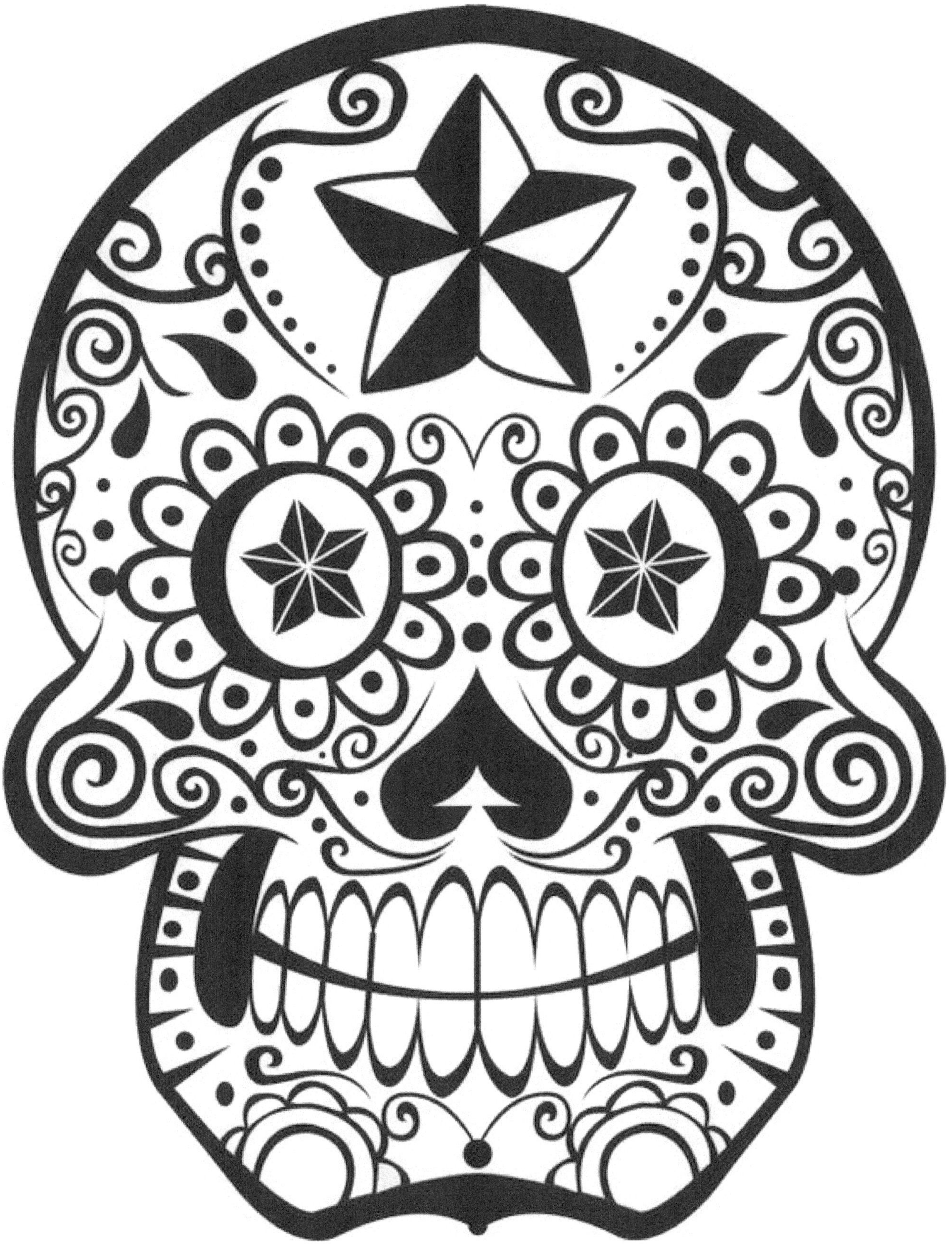

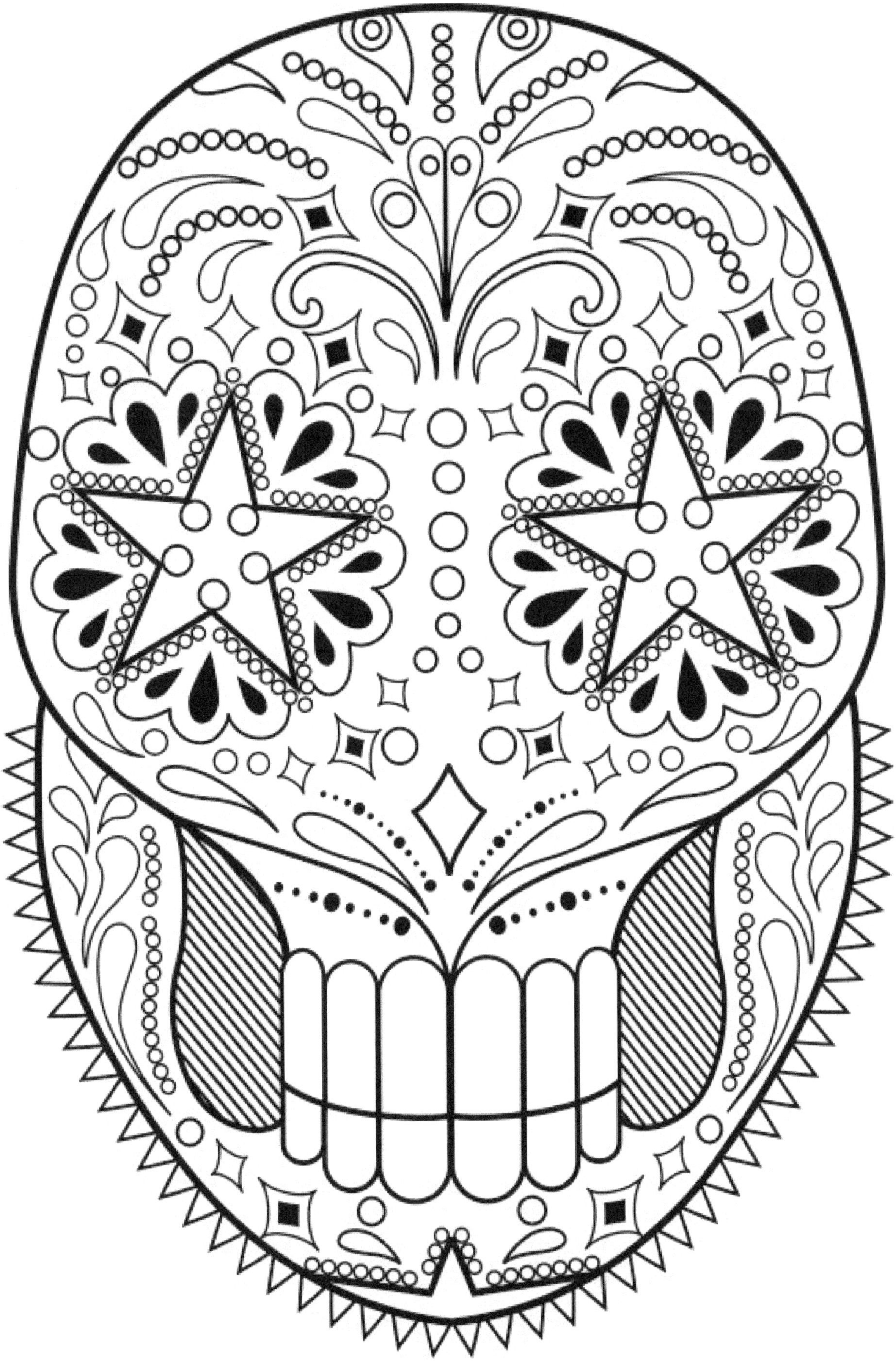

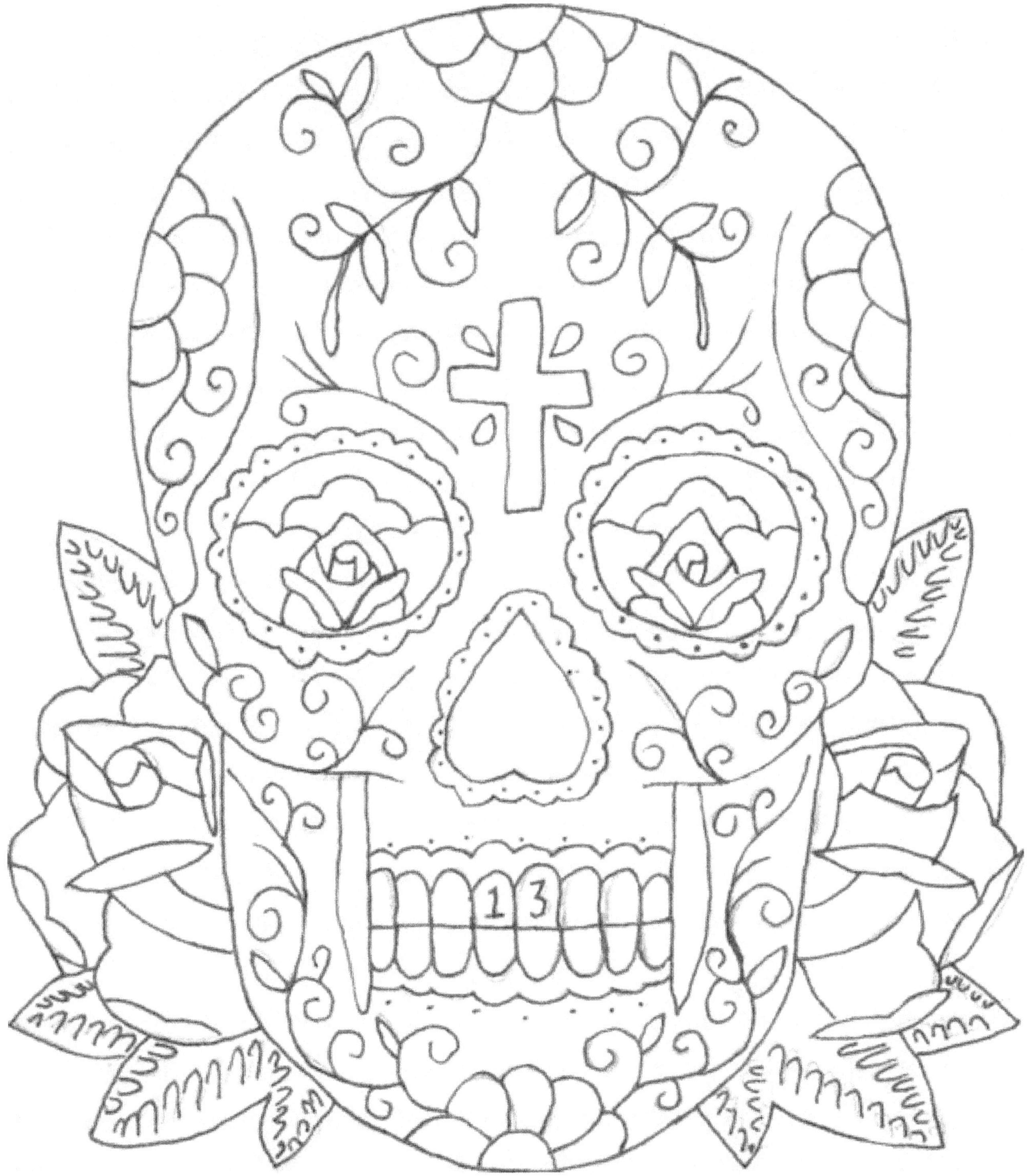
13

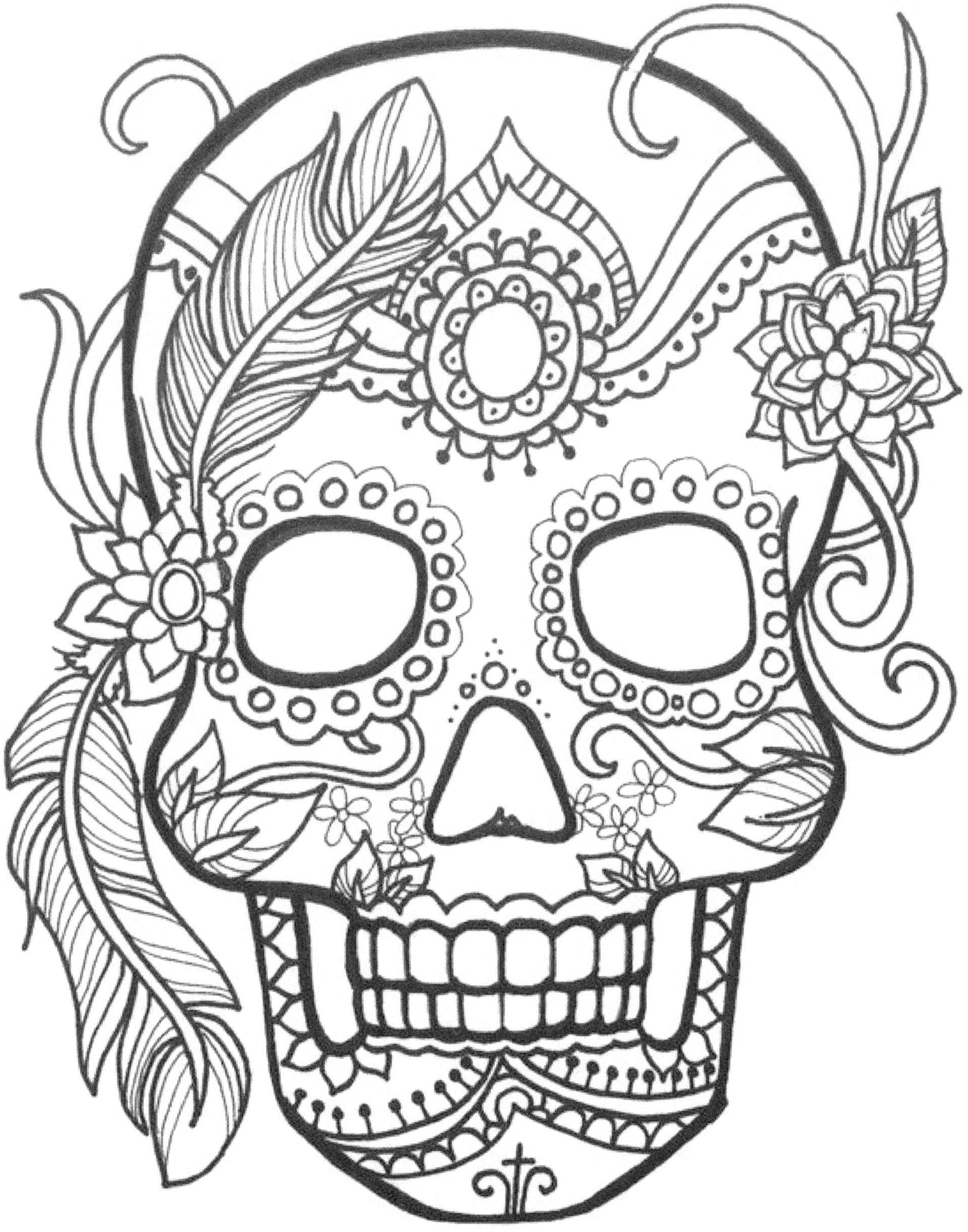

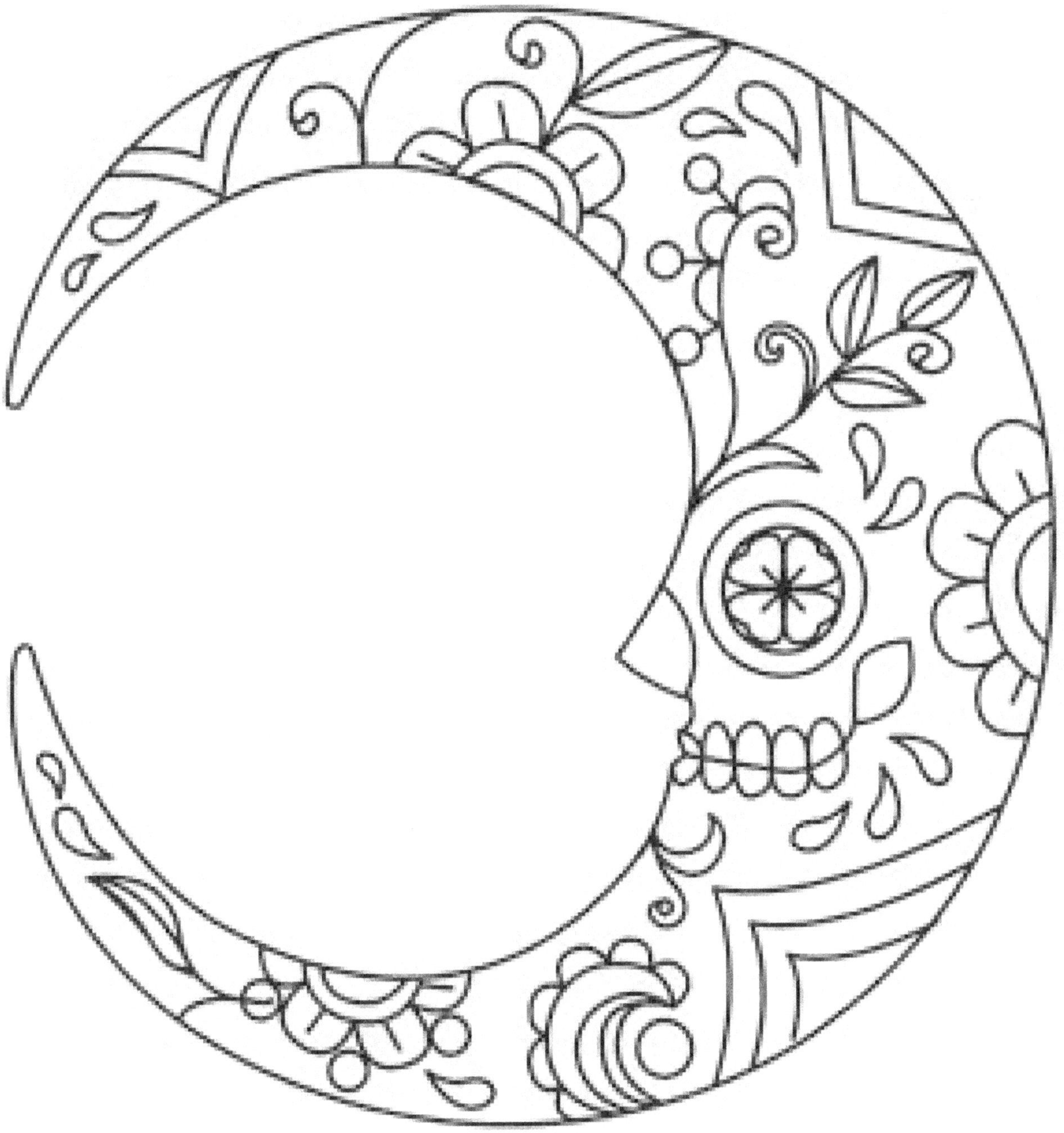

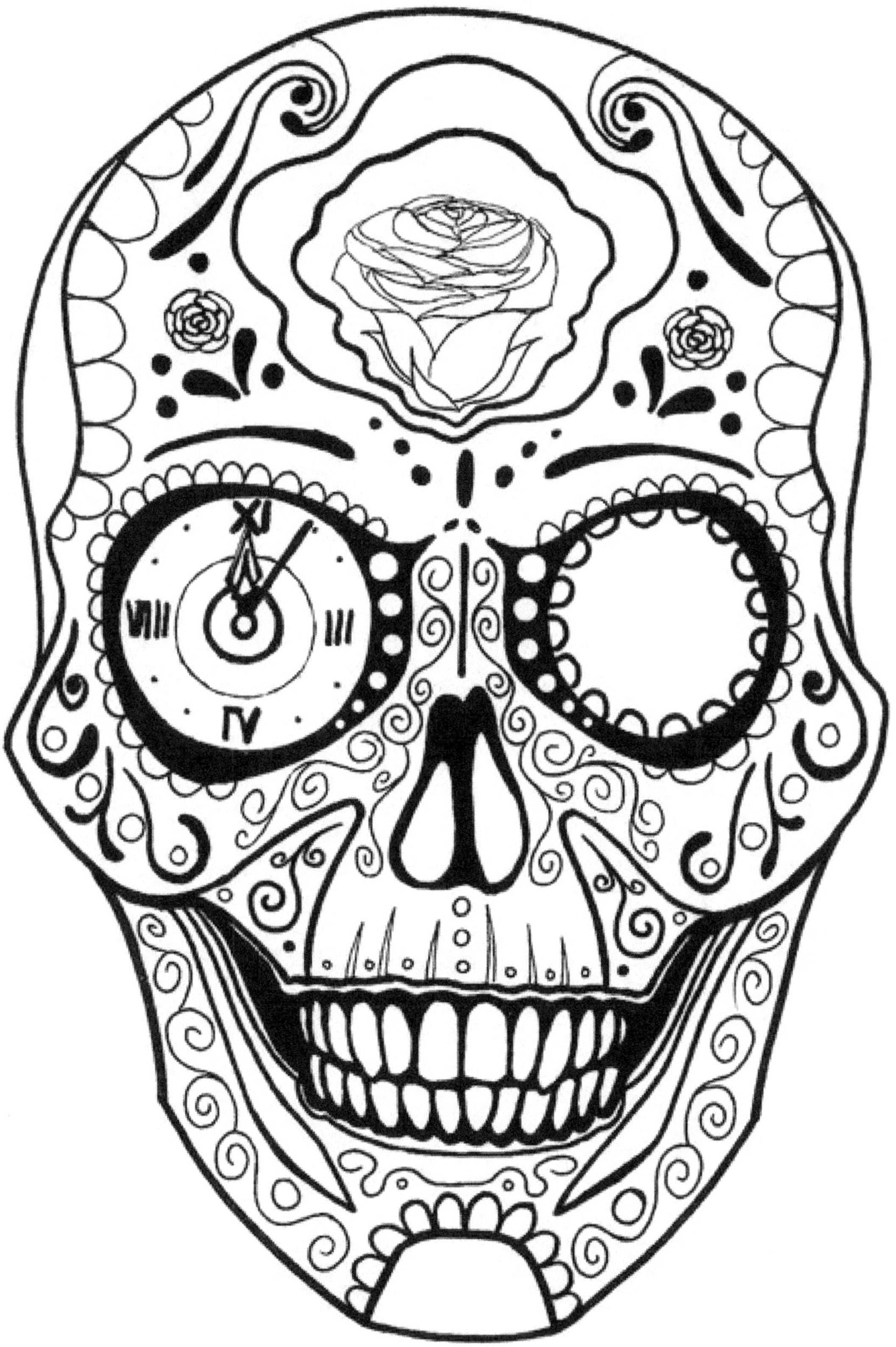

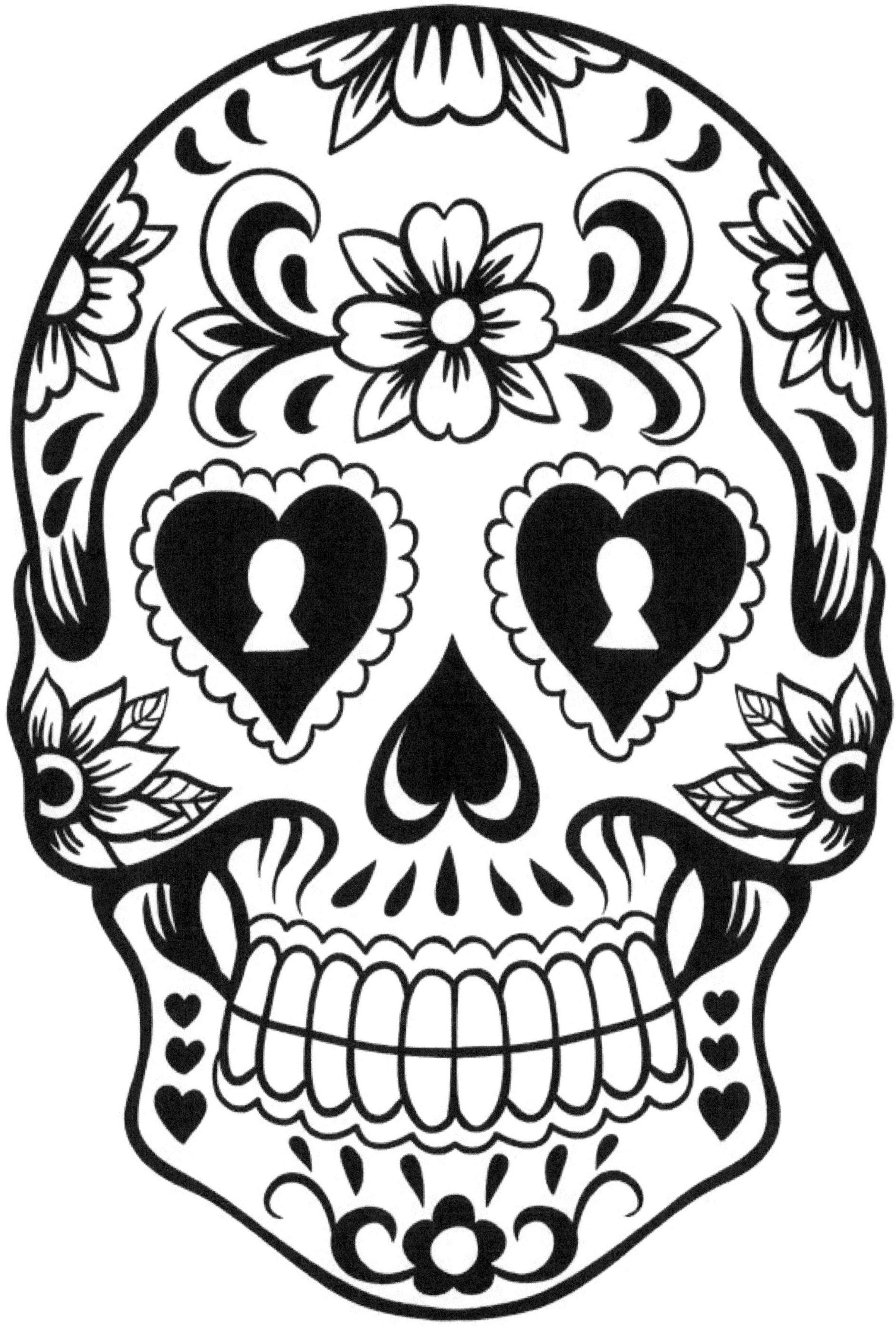

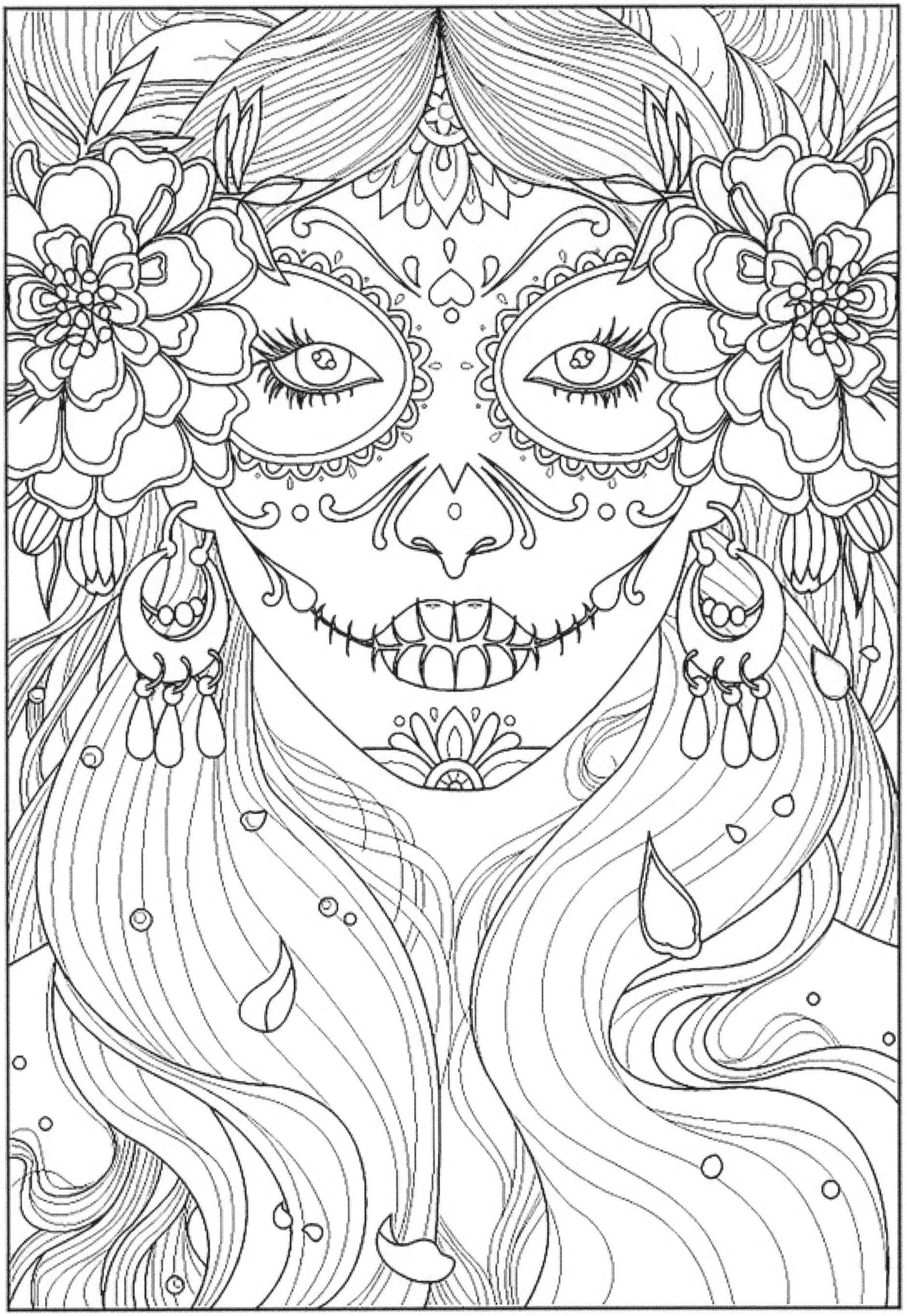

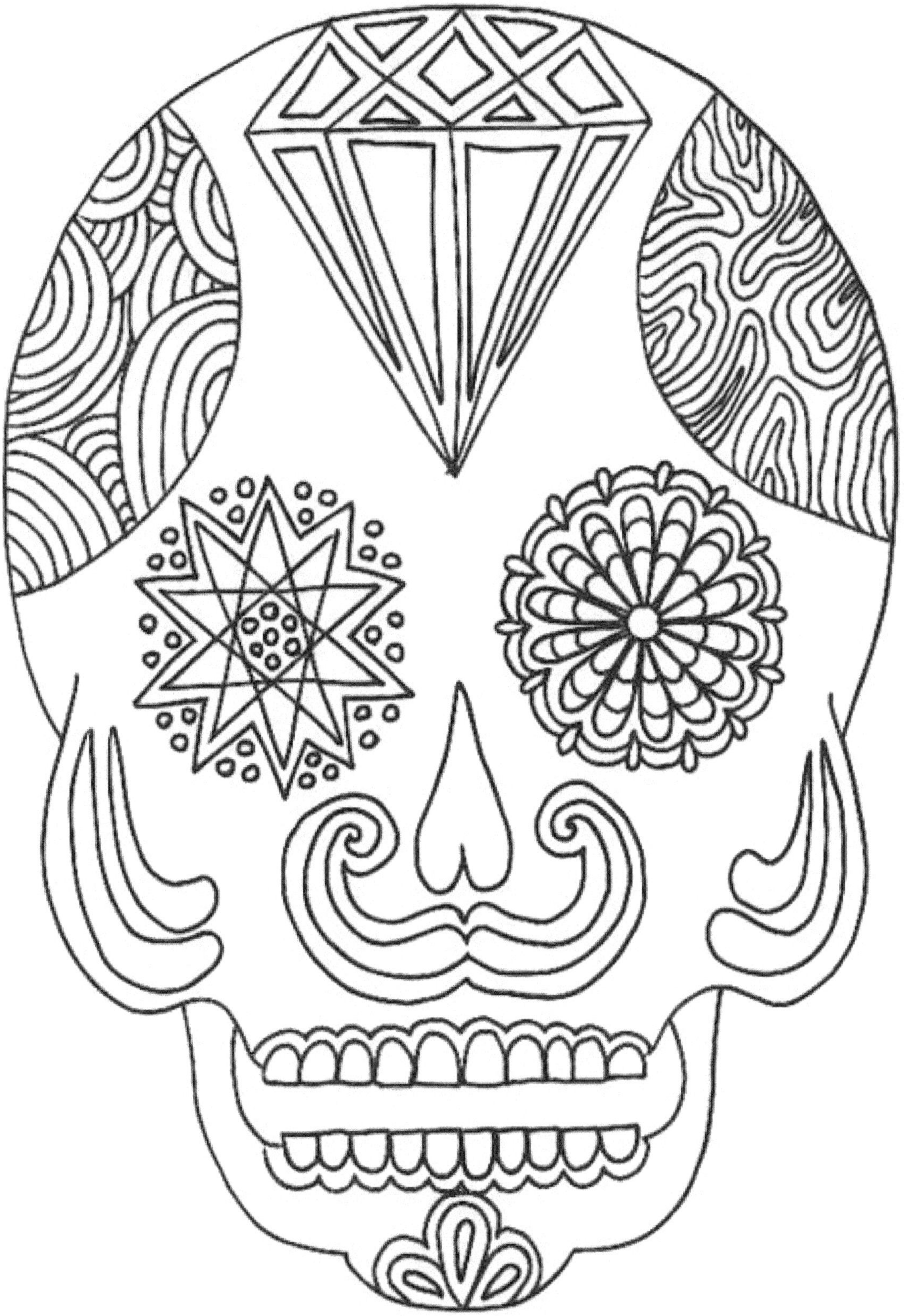

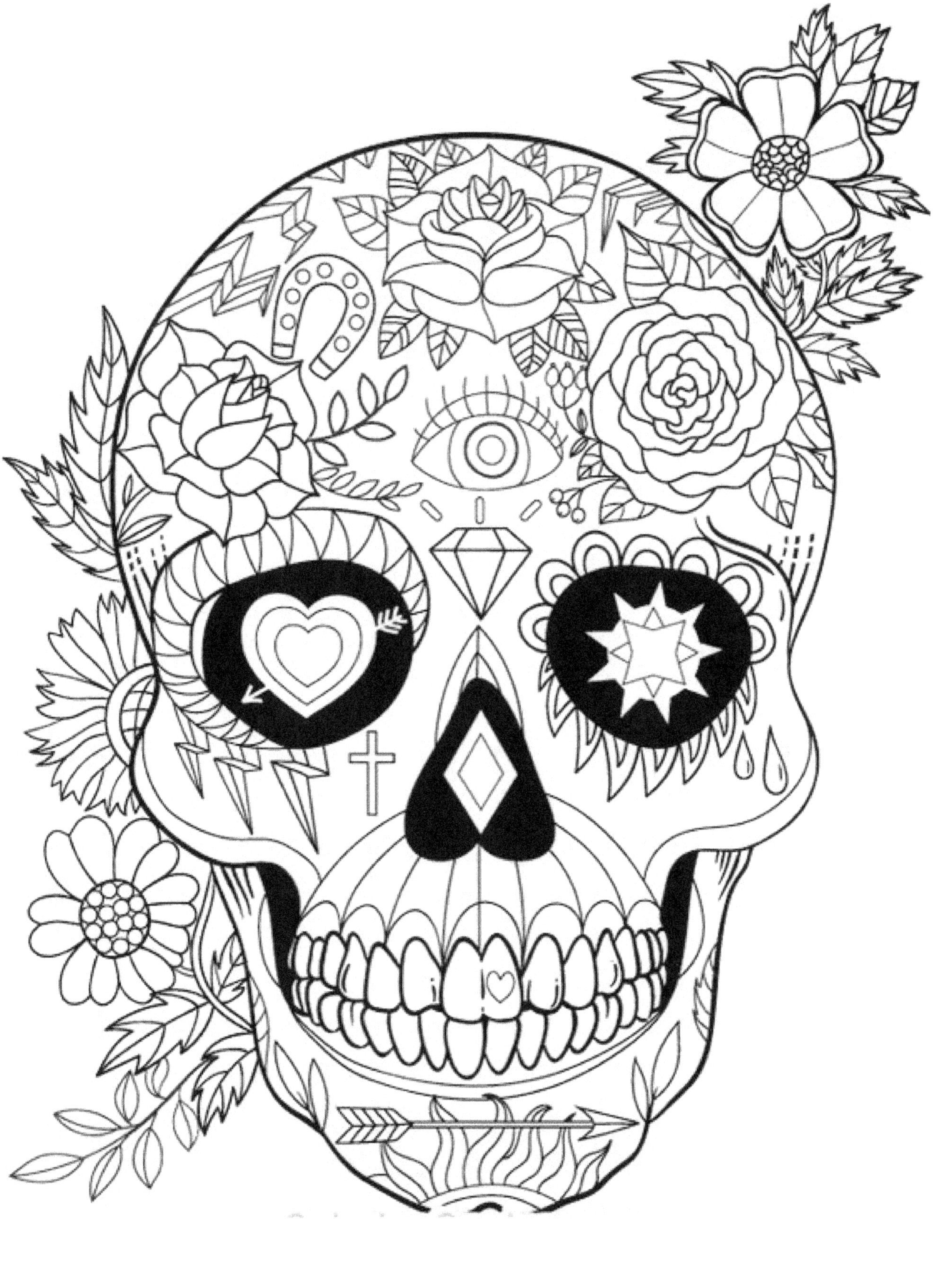

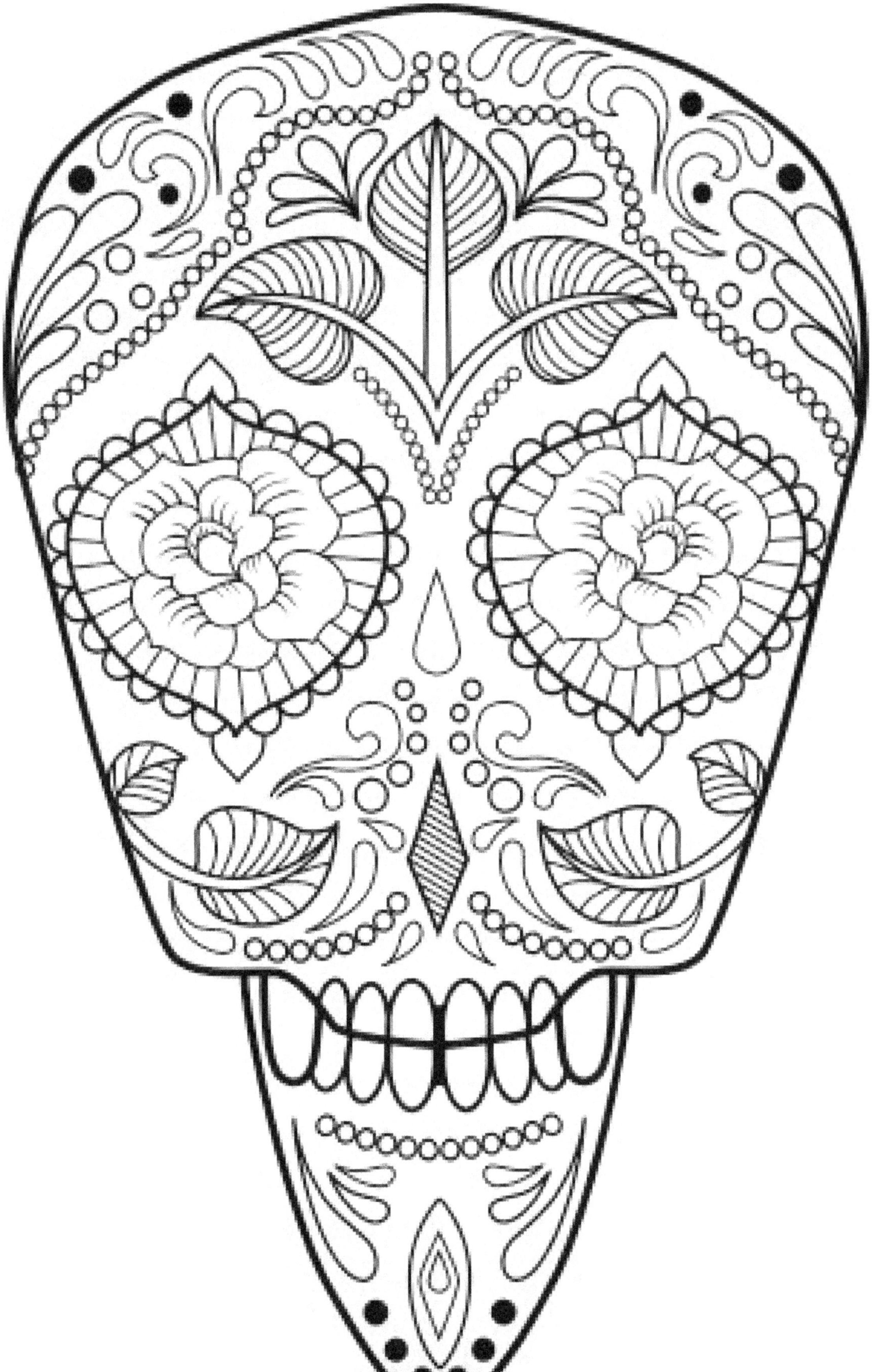

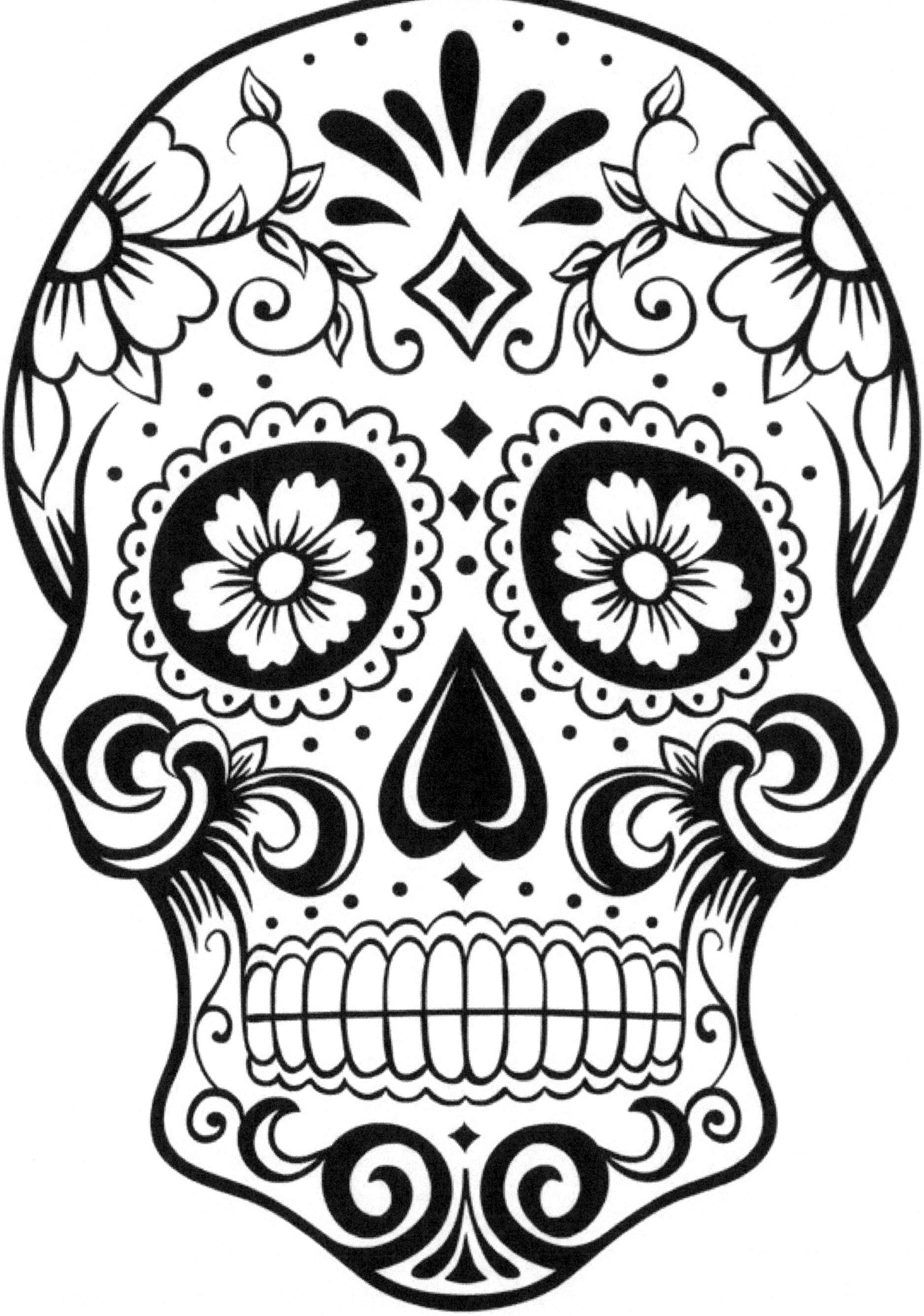

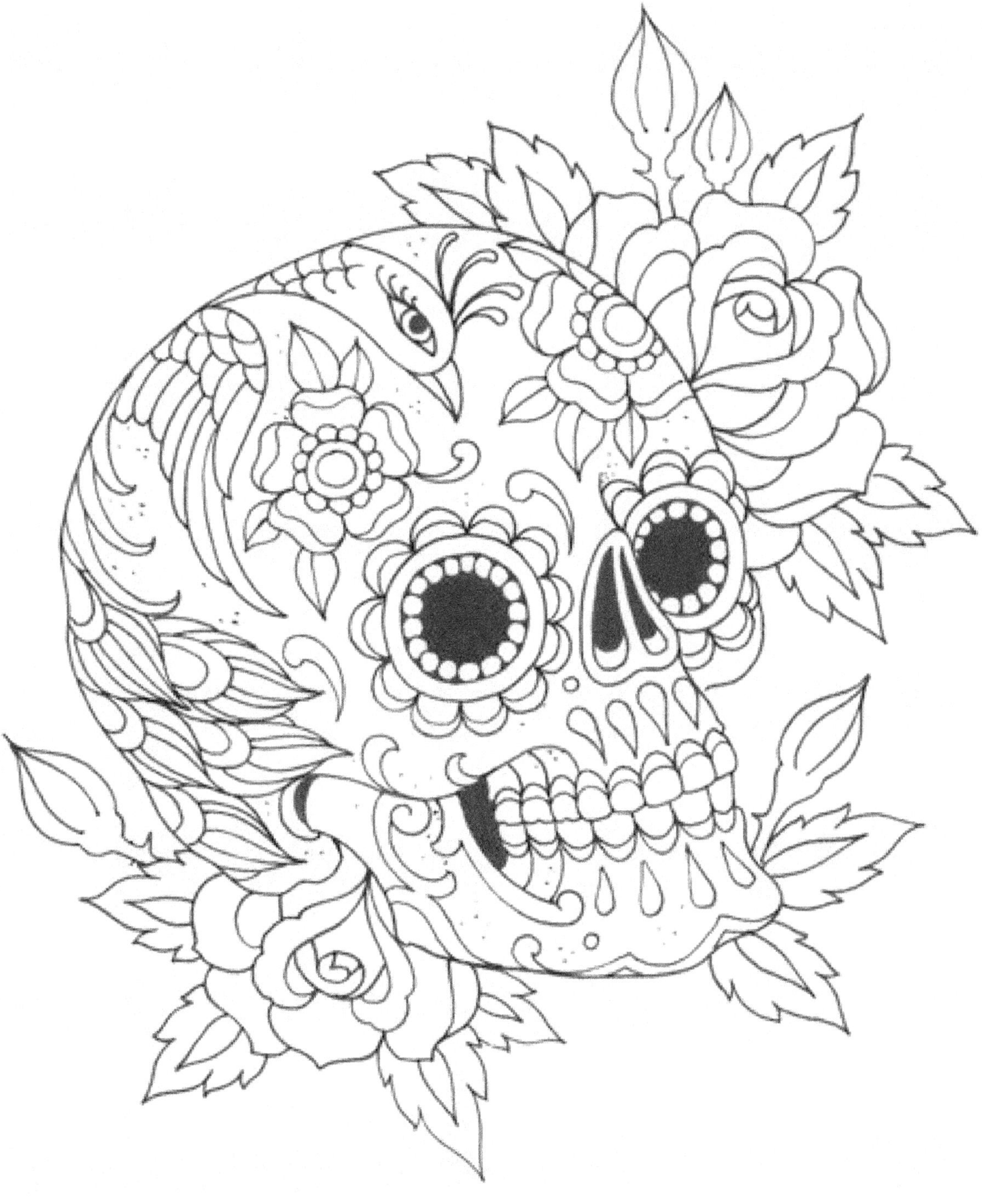

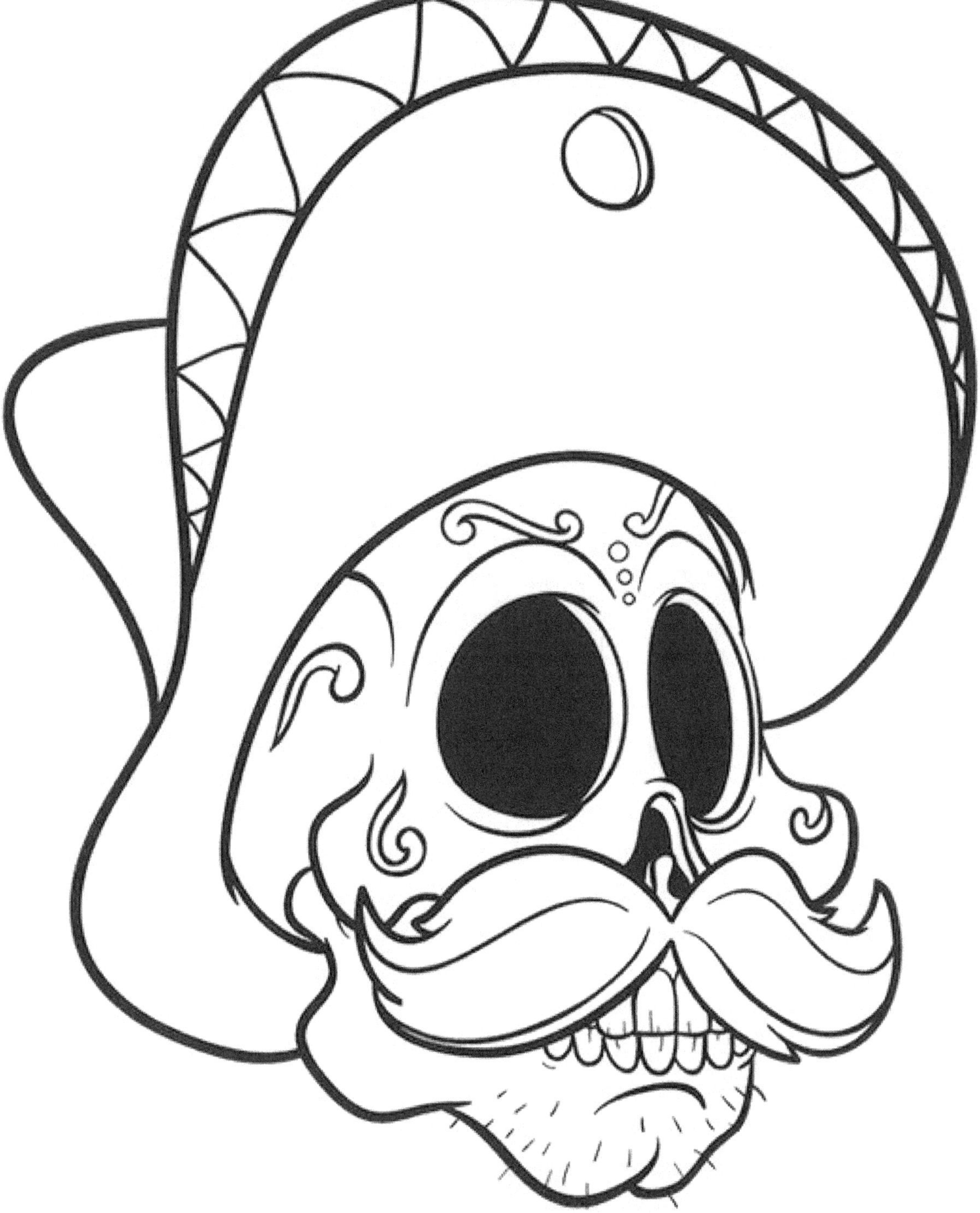

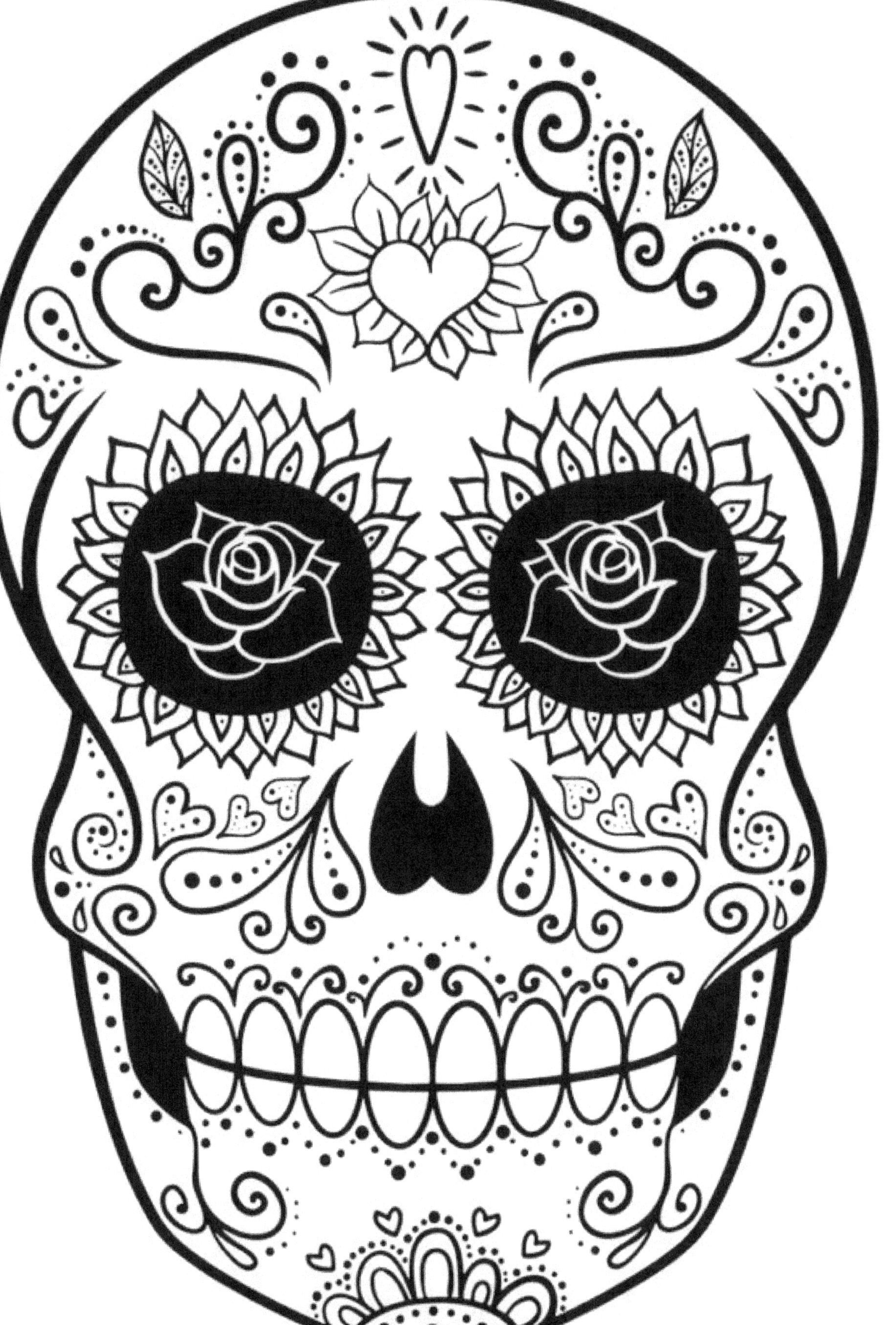

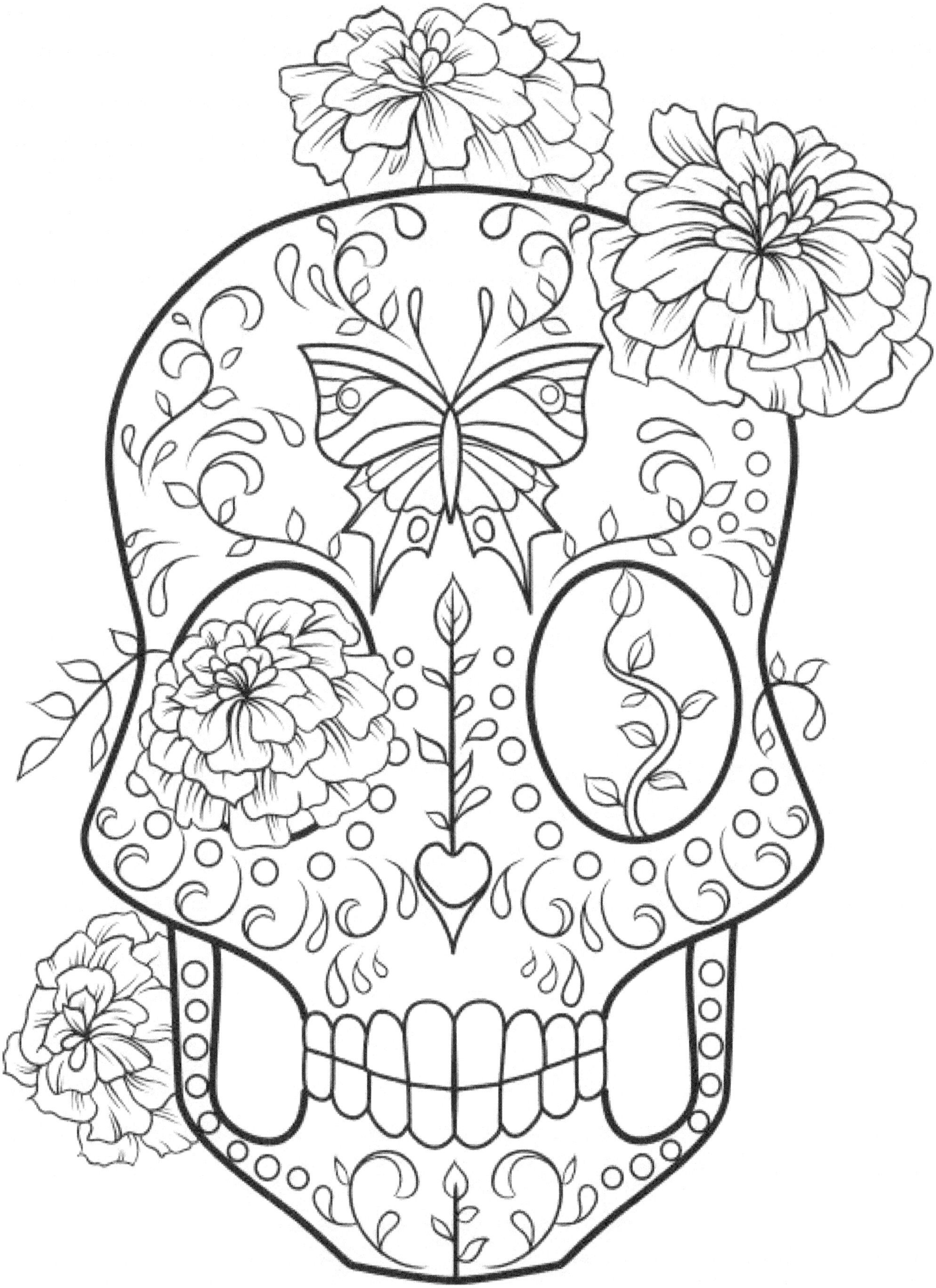

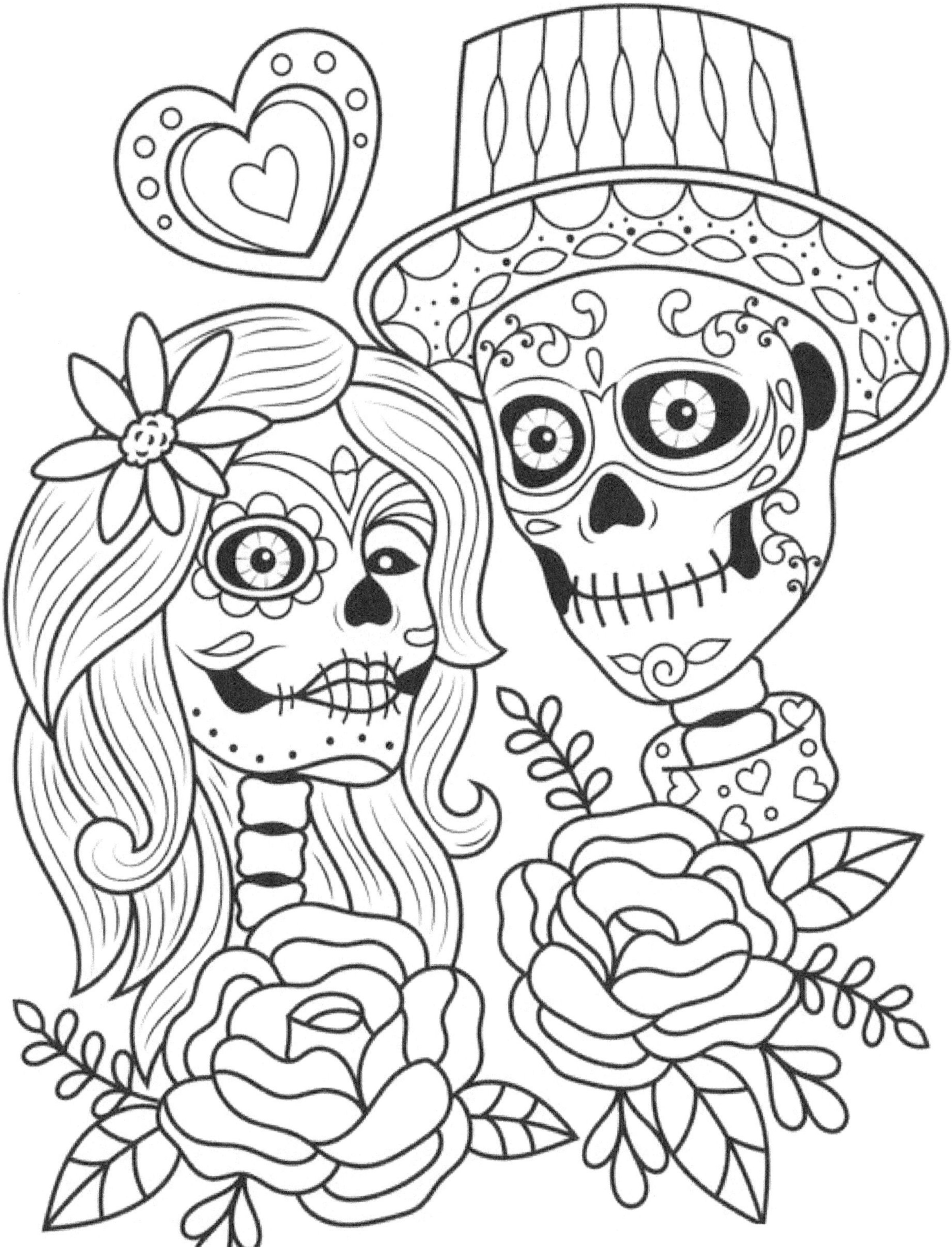

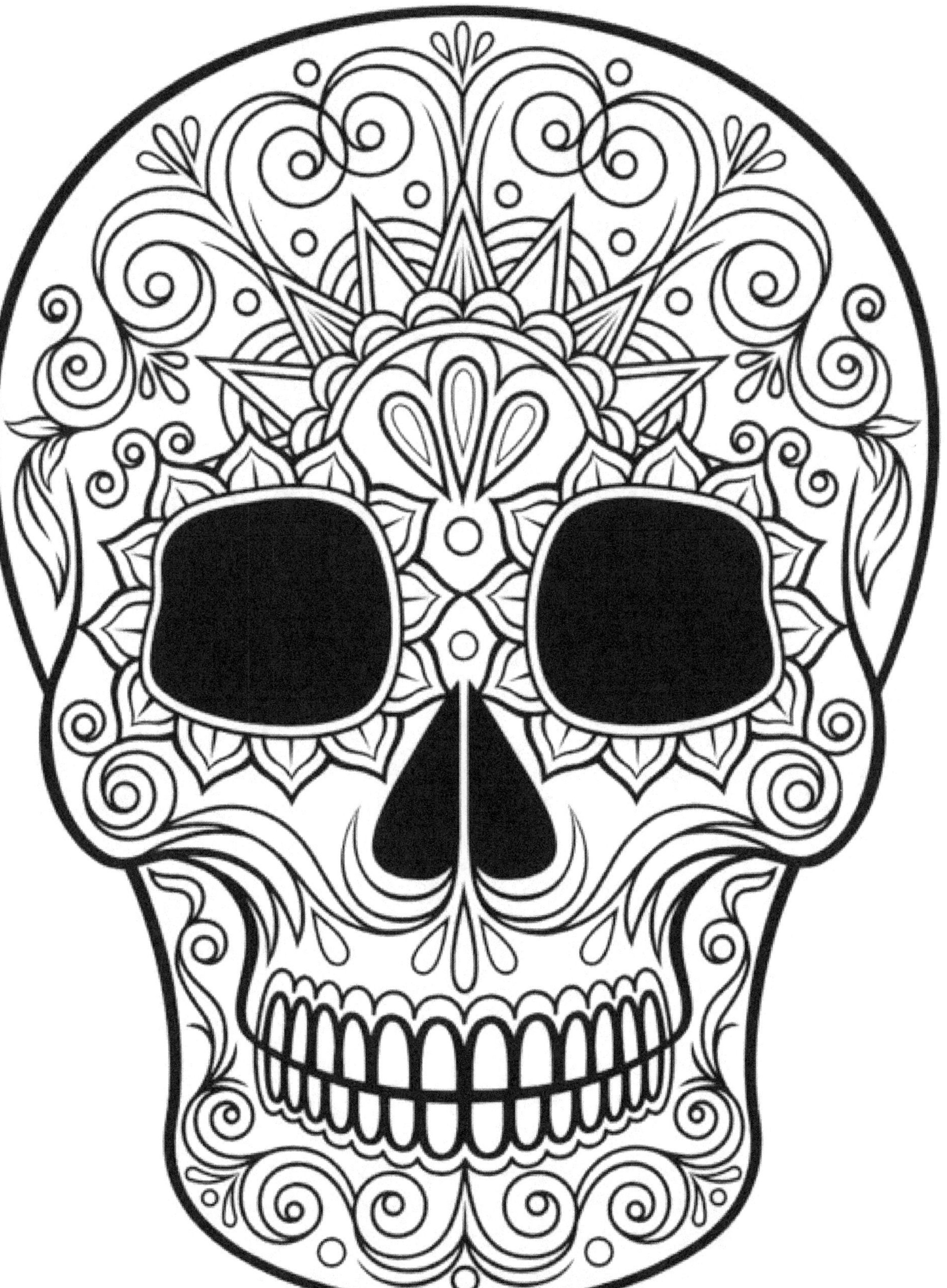

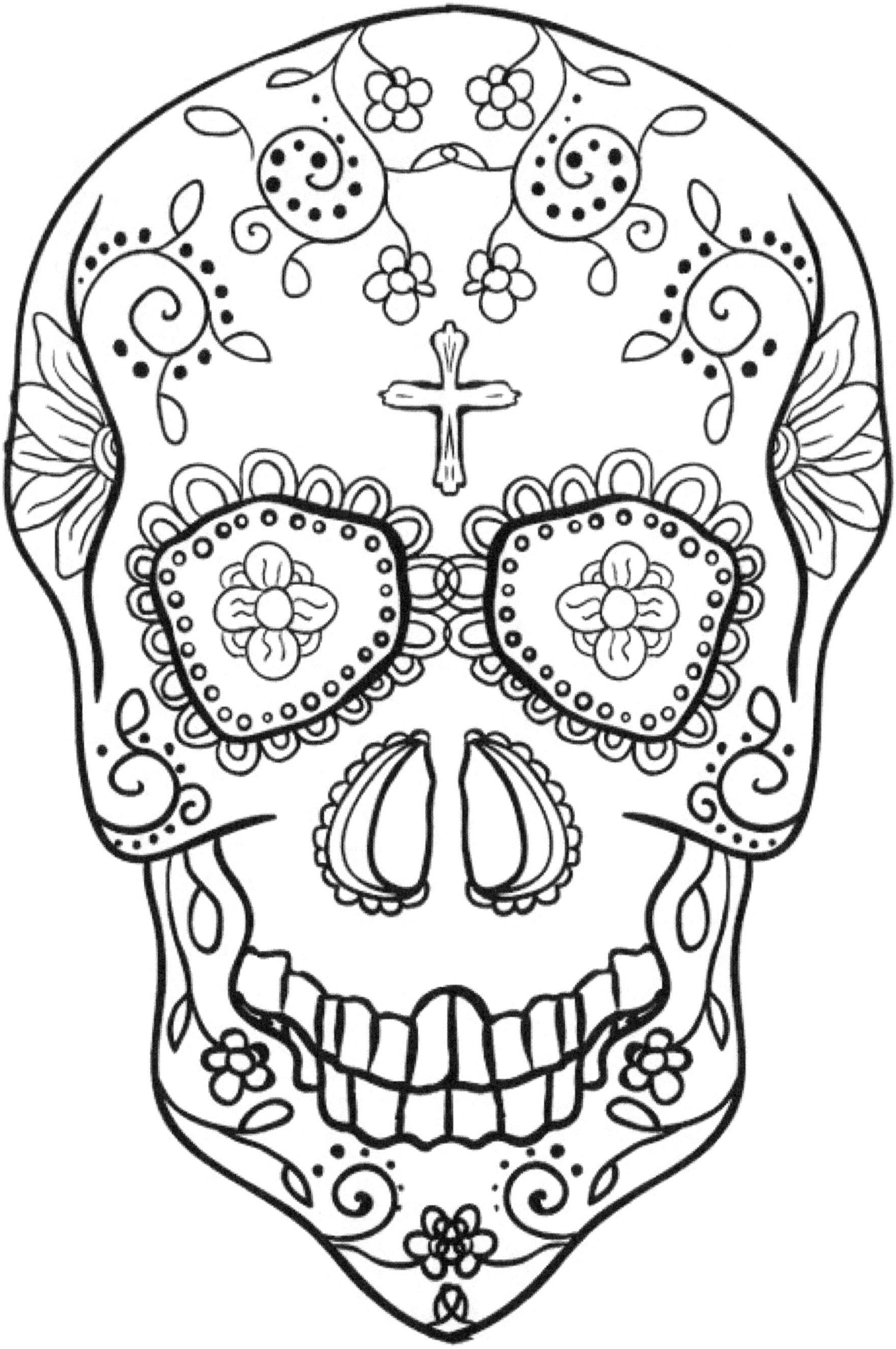

Copyrighted Material

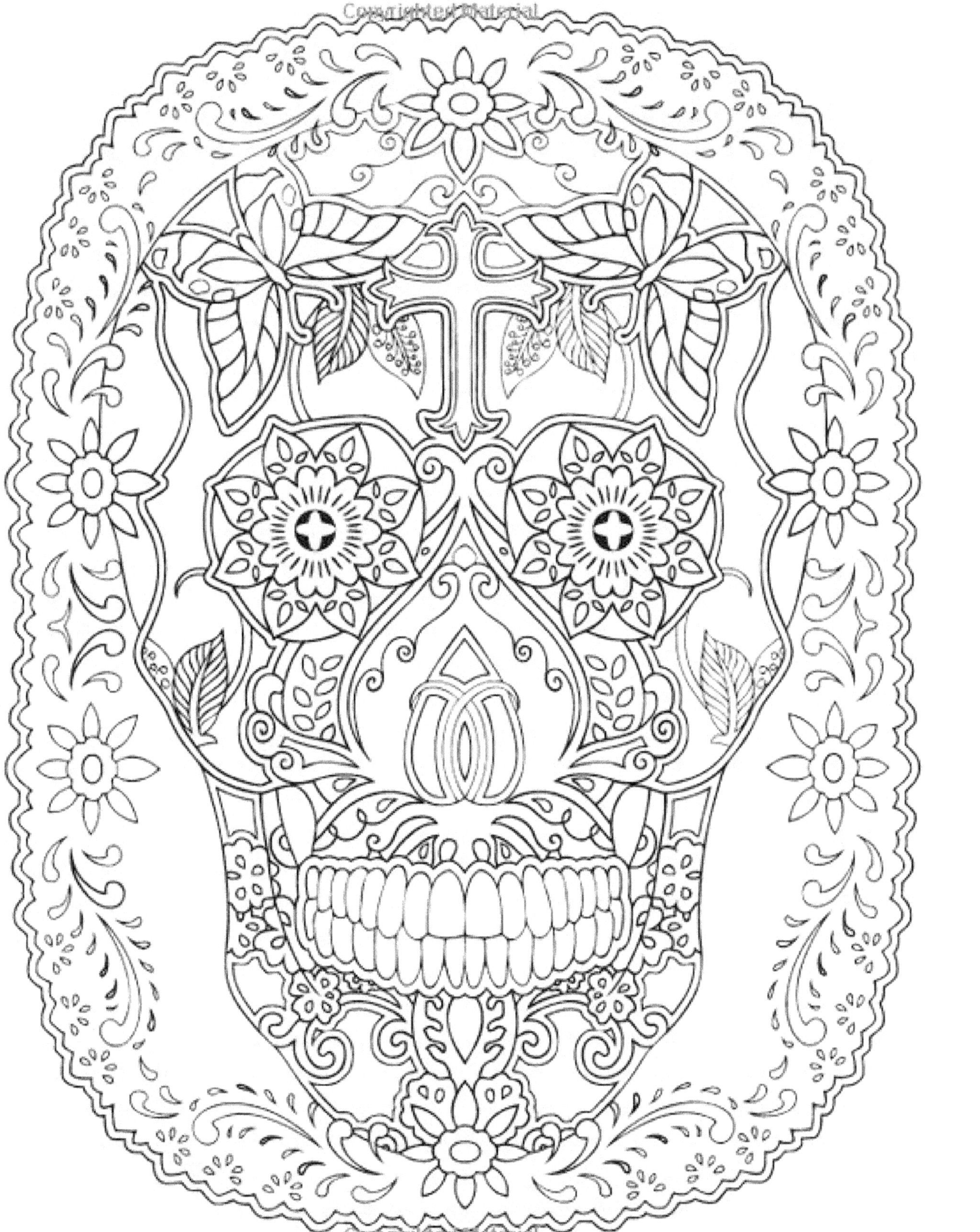

Copyrighted Material

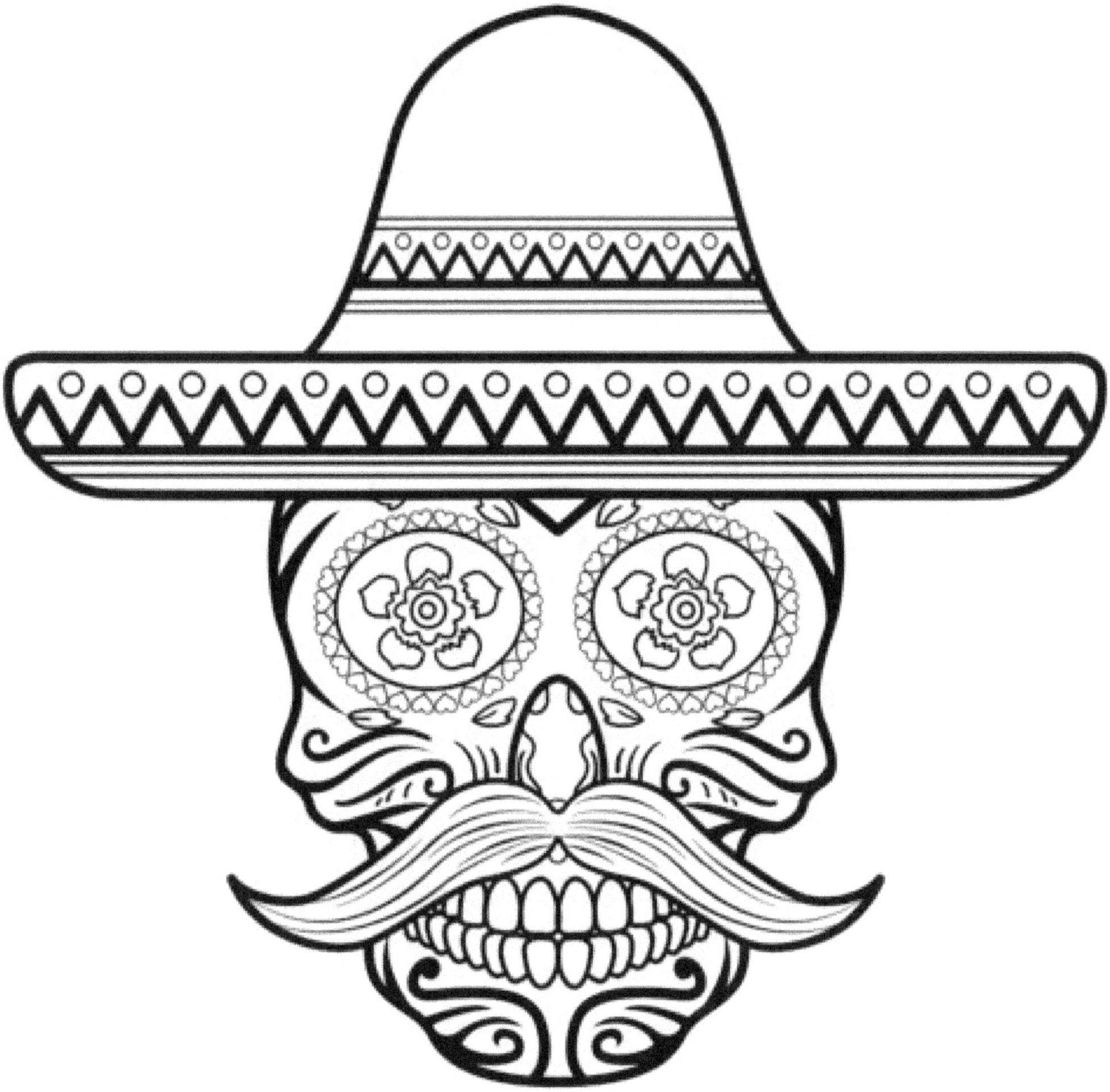

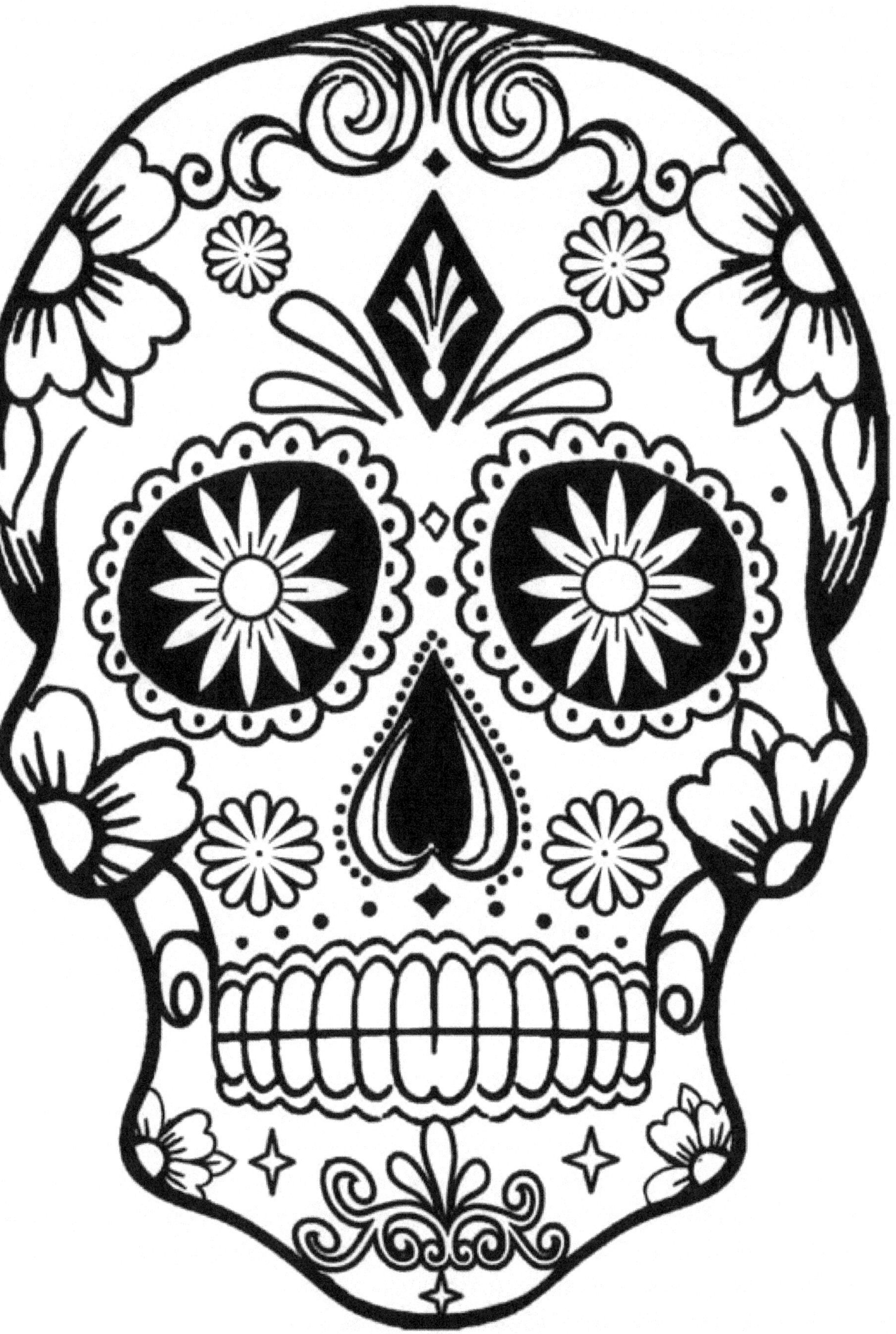

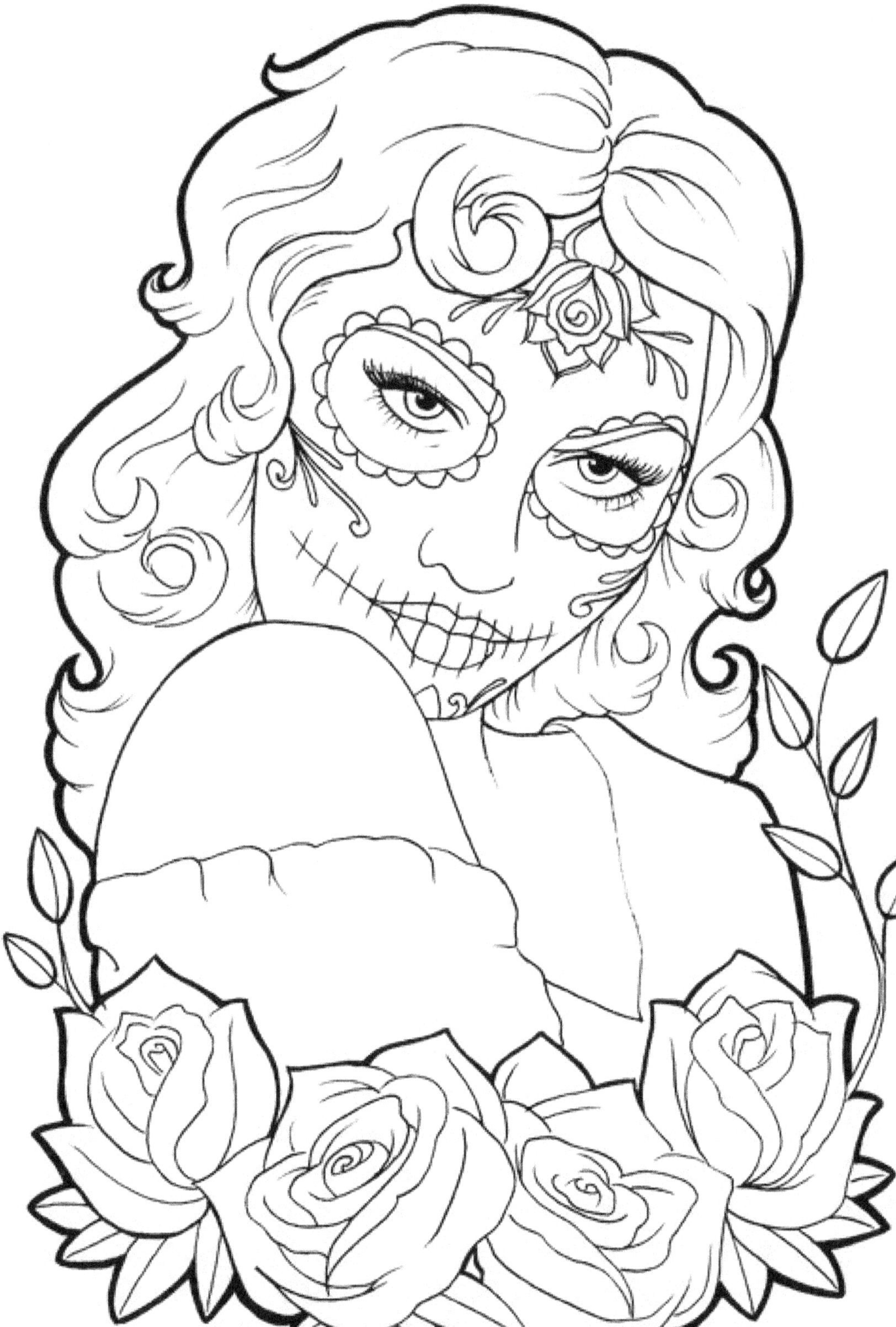

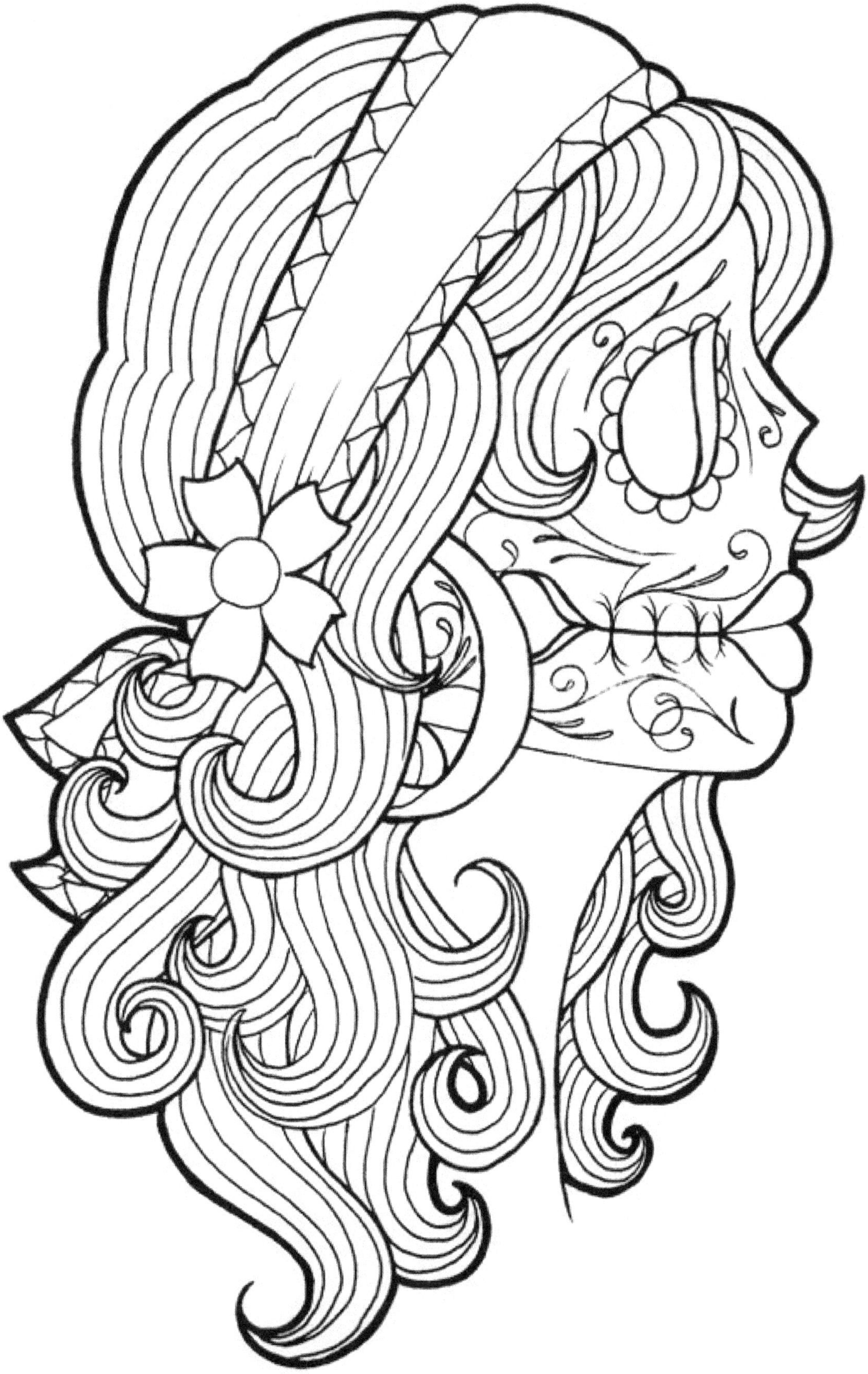

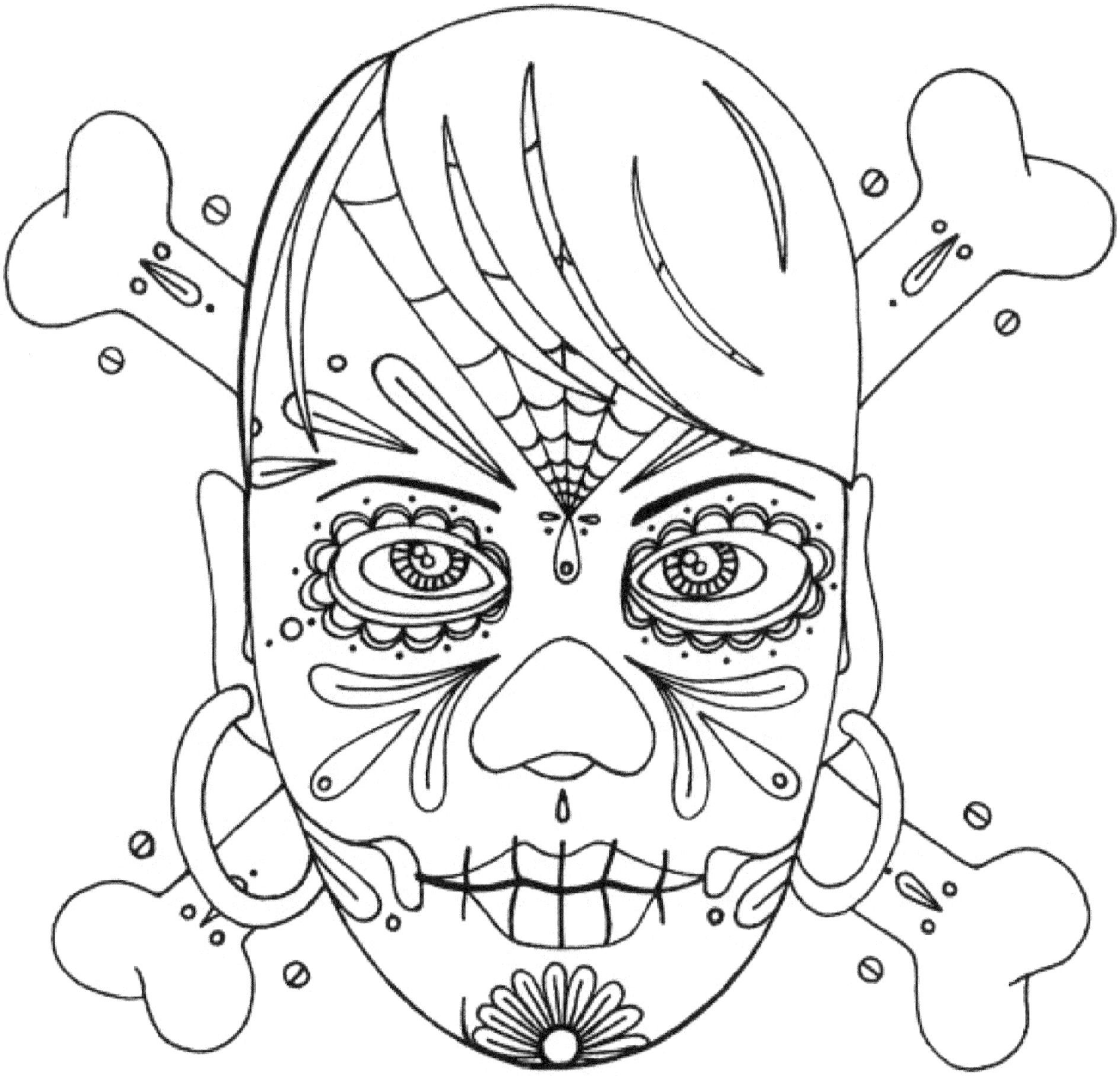

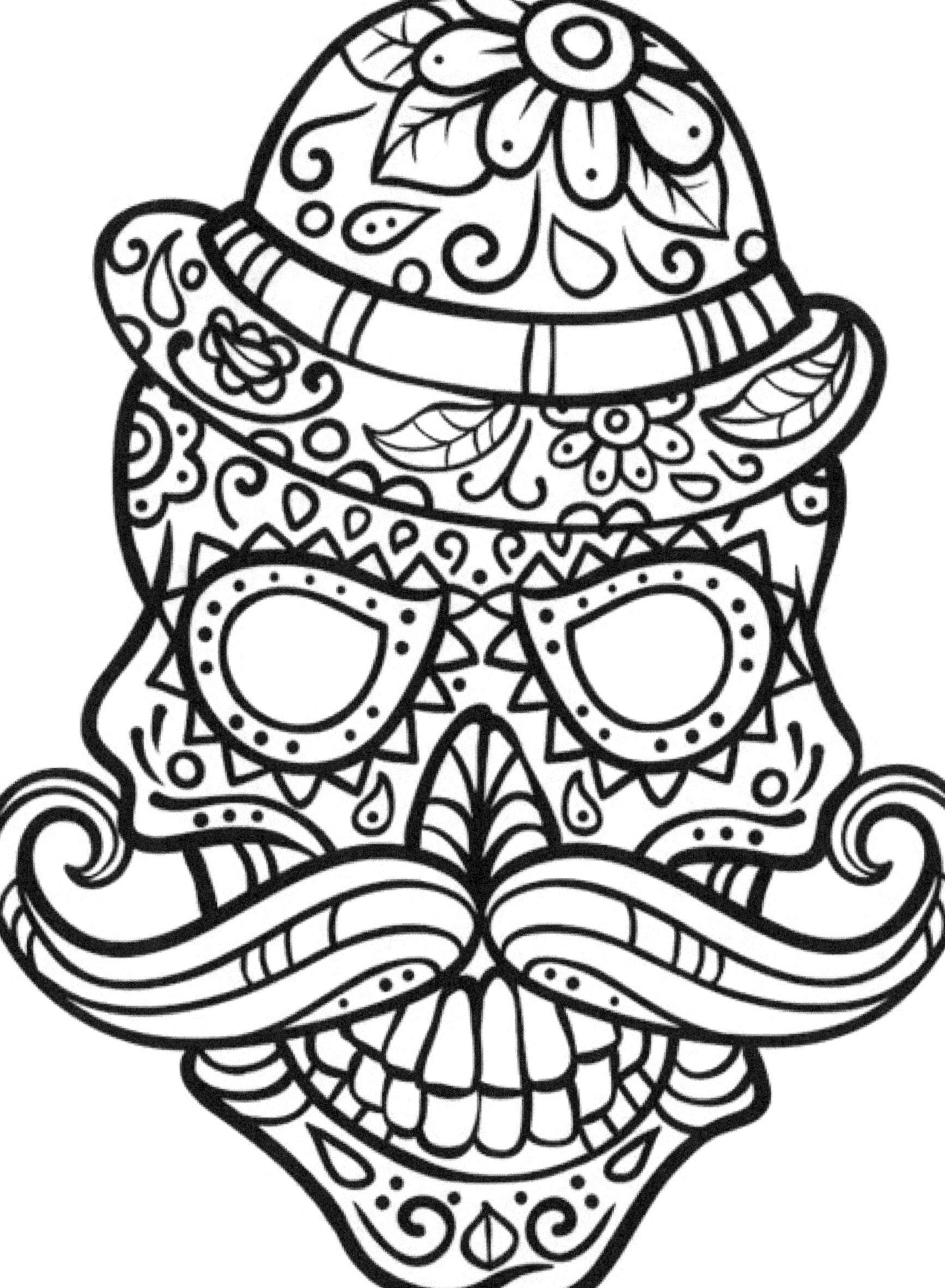

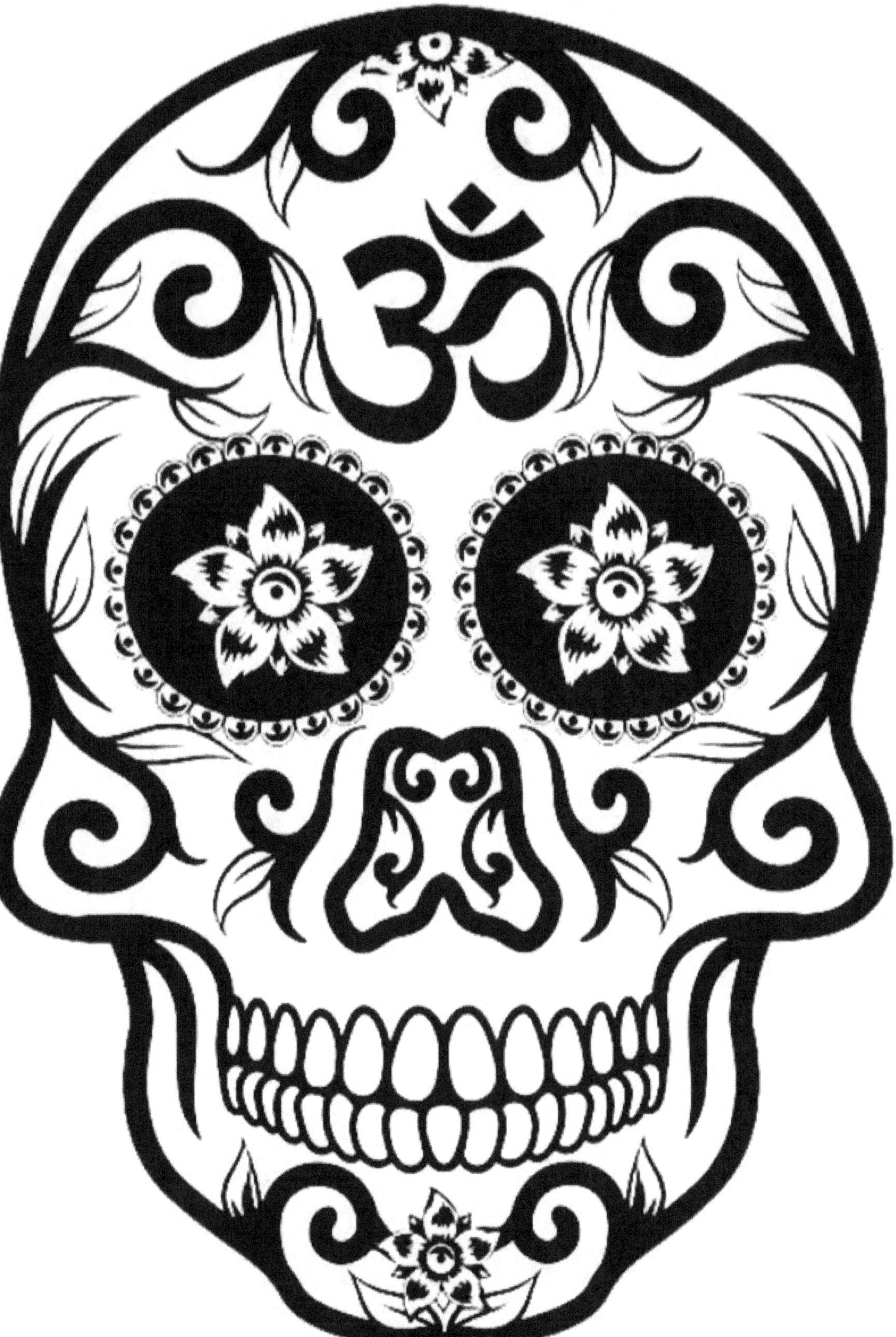

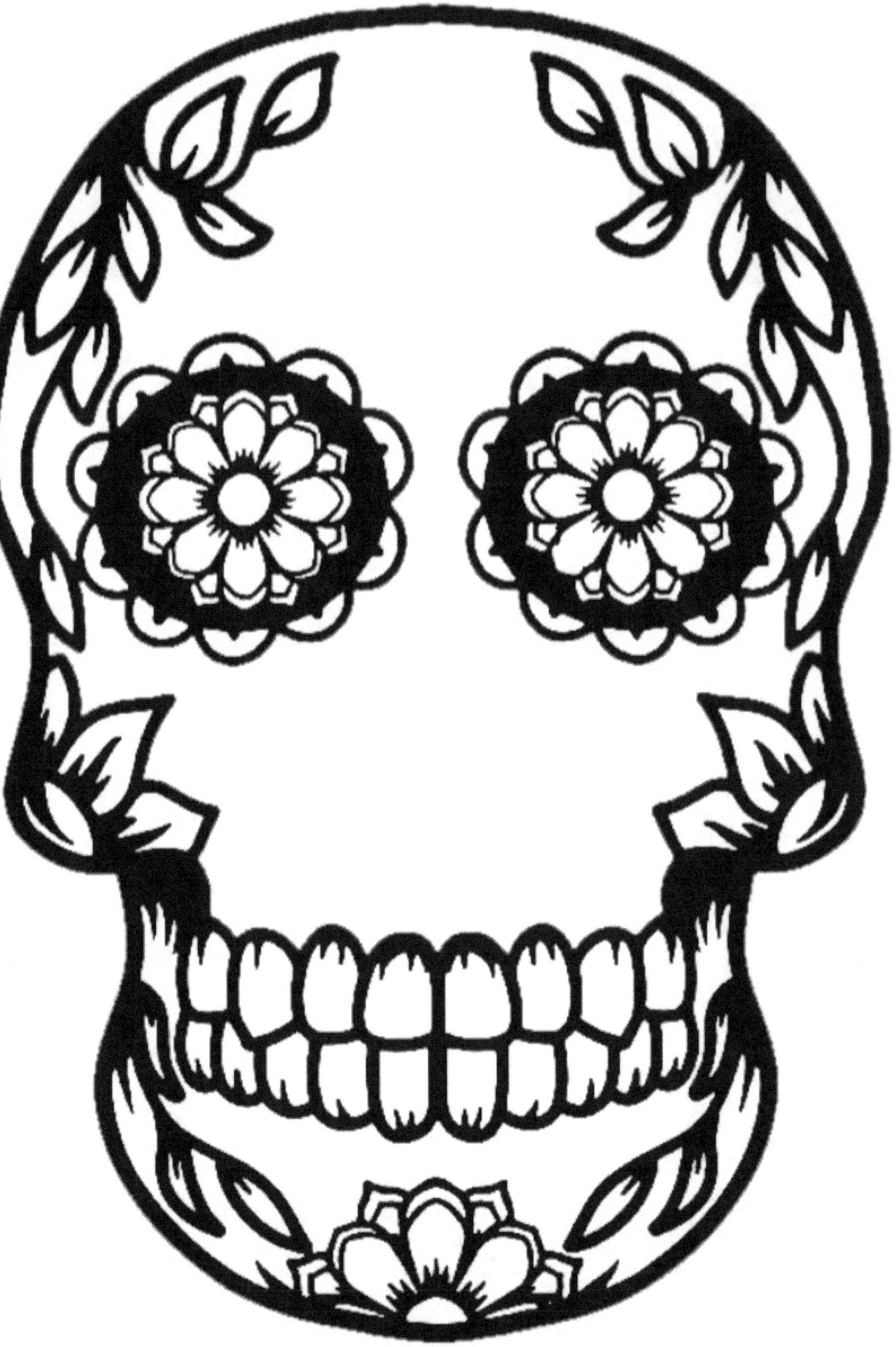

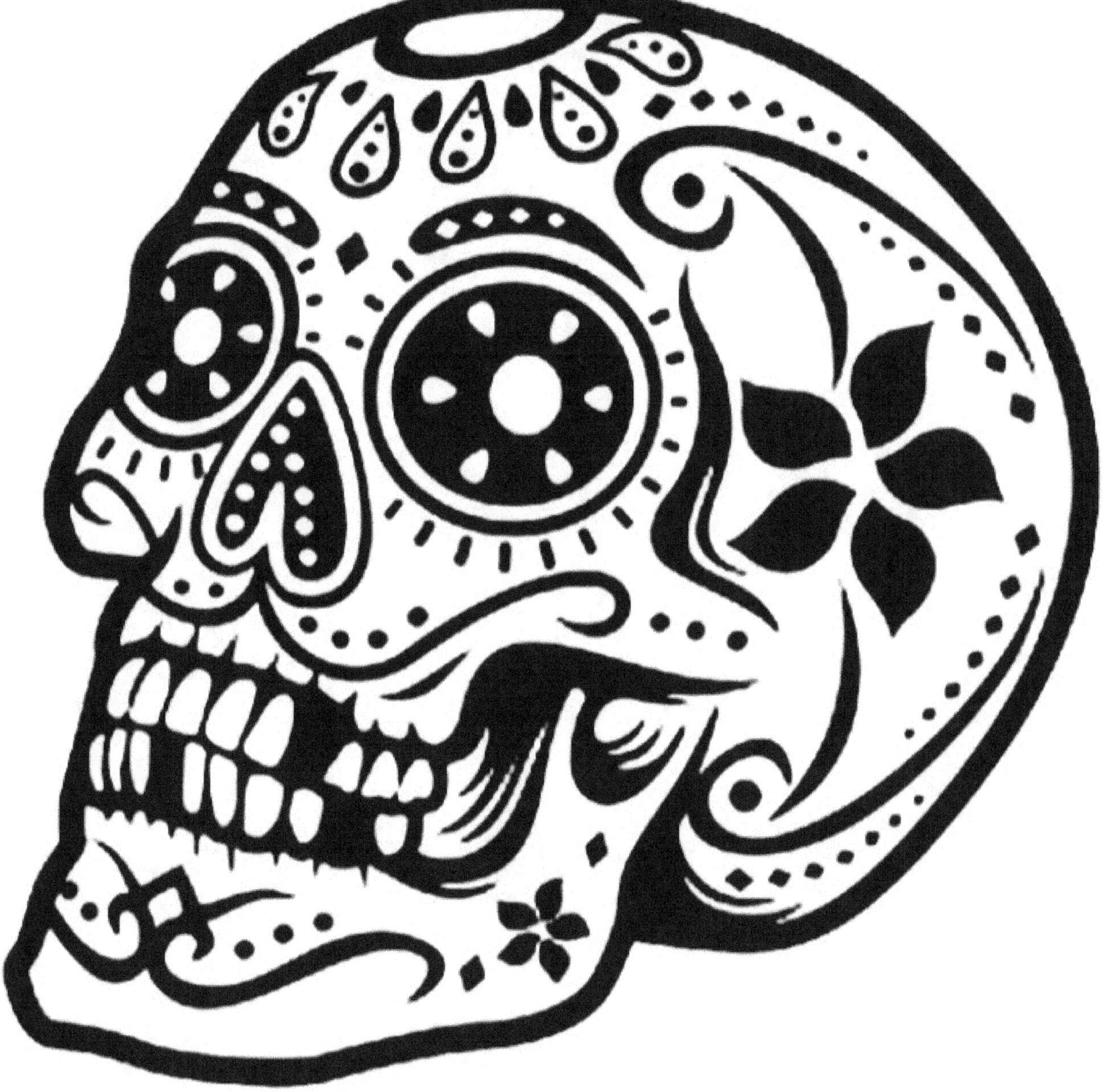

www.ingramcontent.com/pod-product-compliance
Lightning Source LLC
Chambersburg PA
CBHW080849220526
45467CB00008B/2449